how2become

Law National Admissions Test
(LNAT)

www.How2Become.com

As part of this product you have also received **FREE** access to online tests that will help you to pass the LNAT.

To gain access, simply go to:

www.PsychometricTestsOnline.co.uk

Get more products for passing any test or interview at:

www.how2become.com

Orders: Please contact How2become Ltd, Suite 2, 50 Churchill Square Business Centre, Kings Hill, Kent ME19 4YU.

You can order through Amazon.co.uk under ISBN: 9781910602201 via the website www.How2Become.com or through Gardners.com.

ISBN: 978-1-910602-20-1

First published in 2015 by How2become Ltd.

Typeset for How2become Ltd by Anton Pshinka.

Printed in Great Britain for How2become Ltd by: CMP (uk) Limited, Poole, Dorset.

Disclaimer

Every effort has been made to ensure that the information contained within this guide is accurate at the time of publication. How2become Ltd are not responsible for anyone failing any part of any selection process as a result of the information contained within this guide. How2become Ltd and their authors cannot accept any responsibility for any errors or omissions within this guide, however caused. No responsibility for loss or damage occasioned by any person acting, or refraining from action, as a result of the material in this publication can be accepted by How2become Ltd.

The information within this guide does not represent the views of any third party service or organisation.

CONTENTS

INTRODUCTION TO YOUR GUIDE

INTRODUCTION TO YOUR GUIDE

Welcome to your new guide, the *Law National Admissions Test (LNAT)*. This guide is a comprehensive testing book which will aid you through your preparation for the LNAT examination.

The Law National Admissions Test (LNAT) was first instigated in 2004, and has since been used to assist university admissions into the UK's leading law undergraduate degree programmes. The aim of the test is to identify students who show the highest levels of competence in critical and logical thinking. Unlike other tests, this test is not based on intellectual ability. Instead, the test measures a person's competencies against the requirements of a law degree course.

If you are serious about studying law, you will need to put the time and effort into your preparation, in order to score high marks and pass the test.

By the end of this book, you will be able to:

- Demonstrate the ability to differentiate between inferences, abstractions, assumptions and generalisations by applying logical and critical analysis;
- Demonstrate high levels of critical thinking and logical understanding;
- Demonstrate high levels of reasoning and interpretation;
- Evaluate arguments and author viewpoints;
- Focus on sufficient evidence, to generate adequate support and justification;
- Analyse information to draw conclusions;
- Demonstrate writing ability in the style of an essay-based question, which will require critical analysis, persuasive writing and detailed points of view.

Good luck and we wish you the best with all your future endeavours.

LAW
NATIONAL
ADMISSIONS TEST
(LNAT)

WHAT IS THE LNAT?

The Law National Admissions Test, more commonly known as the LNAT, is a test used by universities to filter through potential candidates prior to accepting their admission. The LNAT ultimately aids universities (who use this form of assessment as part of their selection process), by selecting the best candidates for legal education, from large groups of highly qualified applicants.

Specific abilities and aptitudes need to be assessed in relation to the requirements essential to pursue an academic course in law. Fundamentally, it is a test of aptitude rather than of knowledge. It is not a test that you can simply sit down and revise for. It is a test that requires a mature understanding of social, technological, economical and cultural differences.

The LNAT **does:**	The LNAT **does not:**
• Test candidates' ability in regards to Verbal Reasoning;	• Assess candidates' intelligence regarding the law;
• Assess candidates' ability in Deductive and Inductive Reasoning skills;	• Rely on candidates' knowledge and understanding obtained from previous education;
• Evaluate candidates' ability in regards to understanding, interpreting and analysing large amounts of information;	• Expect candidates to have prior knowledge to the topics used in the assessment;
• Test candidates' ability to distinguish between inferences, generalisations, opinions and conclusions.	• Guarantee a candidates' place at their chosen university.

The LNAT is a test like no other, and is unlikely to contain the type of questions you will have encountered before. This is due to the test measuring a particular set of skills; a set of skills required for law students. The skills required to successfully pass the LNAT, are the skills that are essential to further your legal education.

WHAT IS THE AIM?

The aim of the LNAT is to allow candidates the opportunity to display a set of skills that are highly valued within legal education. Candidates do not need to know anything beyond a general awareness of current affairs in order to perform well on their LNAT. Candidates can assure themselves of the best preparation by keeping up to date with current social, political, cultural and financial aspects of society.

The fundamental purpose of this guide is to ensure that you are fully equipped for the preparation of your LNAT. Here at How2become, we have done our utmost to create a guide packed full of information, insightful hints, tips and advice, and plenty of practice questions for you to work through, in order to help you better your overall LNAT performance.

WHAT DOES IT MEASURE?

The LNAT predominantly combines strategic measurements and analytical approaches in order to provide a solid and rounded impression of a candidate's aptitude and performance. The test is used by universities to go beyond the 'normal' selection process, and provide a more in-depth evaluation of potential candidates.

The LNAT is used to assess the following areas:

- Analytical Ability;
- Reading Skills;
- Interpretations;
- Comprehensive Understandings;
- Inductive and Deductive Reasoning Skills;
- Verbal Skills;
- Strategic Approaches.

WHO IS REQUIRED TO TAKE THE ASSESSMENT?

Anyone who wishes to study an undergraduate law degree at a university who uses the LNAT as part of their selection process, will need to take the assessment.

You should note, candidates do not need to take the LNAT if the university that they are applying to is not a part of the LNAT Consortium.

The LNAT is a requirement for the following universities within the UK, EU and overseas:

UK Universities:

University of Birmingham

University of Bristol

Durham University

University of Glasgow

King's College London

The University of Nottingham

University of Oxford

SOAS University of London

University College London (UCL)

Non-UK Universities:

National University of Ireland (NUI), Maynooth

IE University (Spain)

WHEN SHOULD I TAKE THE LNAT?

The deadline date for the LNAT can vary depending on the university for which you are applying. It is *your* responsibility to make sure that you have checked the relevant deadline information for your chosen institution, and to make sure that you register on time.

It would be constructive to take the LNAT as early in the academic year as possible. This will ensure maximum choice of assessment venue and availability, guarantee that your payment transaction goes through, and of course, meet the deadline for applications. The LNAT is a popular assessment, and many people fail to realise just how many people will be taking the assessment. Be sure to secure your slot by registering your application as early as possible.

You need to take the assessment in the UCAS year for which you are applying to university. Your results cannot be carried over from one year to the next, so it is important to work out all your times and dates prior to booking your LNAT. Making a plan with the important dates so that you have something visual to look at and remind you, is highly recommended. The LNAT only allows you to sit the test once during the academic year. This mean that from September to June, you can only partake in the LNAT once.

After you have booked your placement for the LNAT, you will then be able to update your profile (discussed in the next chapter), by rescheduling, cancelling or editing any changes to your personal information.

WHAT ABOUT EXEMPTIONS?

Generally speaking, there are no exemptions granted when it comes to taking the LNAT. Only in extreme circumstances will a university consider an exemption based on individual circumstance, in need of validation. If you have applied for more than one university, you will need to apply for an exemption to each.

Incidents that may require an exemption, that would be taken into consideration, are listed below:

- There is no test centre in your country;
- A breakout of war, civil conflict, or natural disaster;
- Unplanned hospitalisation.

In the event that one of the above circumstances does arise, a candidate should notify their chosen university/s as soon as possible, and ask to be exempt, providing evidence when required. Under no circumstances shall an exemption be given due to faults made entirely by the individual. A candidate who misses the deadline because they had trouble registering, or they did not find out about the LNAT early enough, or arrived late to their assessment, shall not be granted an exemption. Said candidate would need to wait the following academic year, in order to re-register and repeat the entire LNAT process.

THE LNAT FORMAT

The LNAT is a computer-based test which is conducted and regulated by Edexcel and Pearson Vue; institutions that are renowned for an array of different tests and assessments for both business and educational purposes. With over 500 test centres across 165 countries, this highlights the extent to which universities rely on the LNAT as part of their admissions. Details of test centres can be found at the following web address: www.lnat.ac.uk.

Details of the Test

The LNAT will last for 2 hours and 15 minutes, during which you will have two sections to complete. The first section will comprise of 42 multiple-choice questions, based on 12 comprehensive passages. Each passage will contain 3 to 4 questions. For this part of the assessment, you will be given 1 hour and 35 minutes to complete all 42 questions.

The second part of the LNAT is in the style of an essay-based question. You will be given a choice of 3 questions, of which you must answer **one**. The essay will need to be typed and submitted in an electronic format. You will have 40 minutes in which to complete the essay.

A clear breakdown of the test is formatted below:

Section A	Section B
A computer-based, multiple-choice examination. You will be asked to read a passage, and then answer questions testing your skills. • The test will comprise of 42 questions in total; • You will be given 12 passages, each with 3 to 4 questions to answer; • You will be given 95 minutes (1 hour and 35 minutes), to complete all 42 questions. A mark out of 42 will be given, and this will be known as your **'LNAT score'.**	This section is in the style of an essay. The topics will cover an array of subject matters associated with financial, social, cultural, political, or technological issues. • The test will comprise of three essay questions, of which you must answer **one**; • You will have 40 minutes to draft and write your essay. This section is **not marked** by the test centre and **does not contribute** to your LNAT score. It is used as an opportunity for you to engage in a subject matter and make a compelling argument.

The LNAT is vastly growing in popularity. The test intends to improve selection processes for universities by:

• Identifying applicants with the correct skills and mind-set for aspiring law students;

• Providing objective evaluations of candidates from a wide range of social, cultural and educational backgrounds; making the system fairer and more diverse.

Below you'll find two screenshots of how your LNAT assessment will appear.

Multiple-Choice Section - Screenshot

SECTION A

One of the bestsellers in erotic fiction draws upon a mixture of romance, passion, power, lust and fantasy. One of the biggest themes of current feminist beliefs, is to champion the idea that a woman's body is her own possession, and what she does with it is up to her. It is a consensual feeling for feminists to believe power is being wrestled from us. However, by buying in these fictional concepts of love, passion and relationships, we surrender our freedom and our body.

Question 2. In author C's paragraph, the term "champion" is used to…

A – Support the claim of a woman's body is her own possession.

B – Reject the claim that a woman's body is her own possession.

C – Challenge the claim that a woman is in charge of her own body.

D – Challenge the feminist perspective of the female body.

Essay Section - Screenshot

SECTION B

1. "Arranged marriages should no longer be tolerated within Western societies". Discuss.

2. Should abortions be made illegal for everyone?

3. Does home-schooling damage children's social skills?

As human beings, it is in our nature to find our own life partner through freedom of choice.

On the Day

On the day of your LNAT it is important to remain focused, pay attention to the information that you are given, and remember to bring with you the required documentation. This will include:

1. Photo identification.
    a. A current signed passport;
    b. A current signed photo card of your driving license;
    c. A current identity card issued by the Government of the country where the test centre is located.
2. A printed copy of your confirmation letter, sent to you via email.

Please note, the name and date of birth on your photo identification *must* match the name and date of birth that you are registered with. If you do not possess any of these forms of identification, other types of identification may be accepted. Please see the official LNAT website for further details: www. lnat.ac.uk.

Failure to bring any of the required documents will result in your inability to sit the test on that day. Consequently, you would then have to re-book and pay for another place, on another day.

THE LNAT RESULTS

In regards to your LNAT results, they will be available to your chosen university or universities, within 24 hours after completion. Your chosen universities will have access to your results before you.

The LNAT results will be emailed to you on one of two dates, depending on when you sit the assessment in the academic year.

- Candidates who take the LNAT on or before 15th January, will receive their results in early February;
- Candidates who take the LNAT after 15th January, will receive their results in early July.

The specific dates of when your results are available to you will vary between years.

REGISTERING
FOR THE
LNAT

REGISTRATION

You need to make sure that the year in which you take the LNAT, is for the same year you are applying to university. LNAT scores cannot be carried on to the following academic year.

After you have familiarised yourself with the process of the LNAT, and worked out the deadlines for which you are working towards, you will then need to register your application online. This is a simple and quick process and can be completed through the official LNAT website: www.lnat.ac.uk.

Without registering, you will not be able to sit the assessment. You will receive all of the important information through your LNAT account including: locations of test centres, assessment dates and times, paying for the LNAT, and terms and conditions.

Note that special arrangements can be made for the LNAT if required, and instructions on how to do so can be found on the LNAT website. You should follow these instructions *before* commencing with the process of booking.

Remember to register your account as early as possible to ensure that you are guaranteed a slot that suits you. If you leave your registration to the last minute, you are unlikely to get a slot at your nearest test centre or on your preferred date. It is important that you manage your time and register your account as soon as you can.

HOW TO SET UP YOUR LNAT ACCOUNT

In order to book your place for the LNAT, you need to set up an online account. This is easily done through the official LNAT website.

If you are applying through UCAS, and have received your UCAS identification number, you will need this to register. However, if you have applied to sit the LNAT before your UCAS number is provided, you are still able to apply. All you will need to do is edit your profile and enter your UCAS personal identity number once you receive it. Your UCAS number will be needed by your chosen institution, so you *must* remember to edit and update your personal details.

Who Can Register?

You can register your application yourself, or you can get a parent, guardian or teacher to register for you. Make sure that if you ask someone else to register for you, that you have checked all the information they have provided is correct. Foremost, it is your responsibility to make sure that a) your account gets registered in time, and b) that the information provided on your profile is accurate.

Providing an Email Address

Providing a valid email address is a crucial part of your application. You will need to use a correct email address, so that you receive all of the correspondence and information regarding details of the LNAT. The email address will also be used to send your results, so make sure that your registered email address is one that you check on a regular basis.

If you do decide to change your email address after registering your profile, then you need to notify the exam board by editing your profile. If you do not notify them of any changes, you should assume that your results and any other information will be sent to the original email address.

HOW TO BOOK YOUR TEST

Once you have created your online account, and have received your LNAT username and password, you are able to book your test.

To book your test, you will need to follow the steps listed below:

1. Log in to your LNAT account using your username and password;
2. Navigate to the menu bar (usually positioned at the top left of the screen) to make a booking;
3. Choose which day you would like to sit the LNAT. The test can be taken on any day that has available slots free at the test centre you have chosen.

You can make a booking through your school or college, but ultimately it is still your responsibility to make sure that you book well in advance of the closing date for applications.

How to Change your Booking

If, for some reason, you are unable to attend the date you have booked, you can reschedule or cancel your test by logging into your account.

Tests can be rescheduled, without charge, up until noon (UK time) two working days before the date of the test. If you do not reschedule by this time, you will be charged.

IMPORTANT DATES, TIMES AND DEADLINES

The most important thing to remember is to research the dates and deadlines of your chosen institutions. Each university has different deadlines, and again, it is your responsibility to work out which deadlines you must adhere to.

Details of deadlines for universities can be found at the following address: http://www.lnat.ac.uk/registration/dates-and-deadlines/.

HOW TO PAY FOR YOUR LNAT

Test fees are required for candidates who are partaking in the LNAT. The cost for candidates for the 2015 submission is £50 for UK/EU test centres, and £70 at a test centre outside of the EU.

The fee is payable online, and must be paid at the same time as booking. Under no circumstances shall payment be accepted after the booking date.

Payments can be made by most credit cards (MasterCard, American Express, Visa) and debit cards. Switch or Maestro credit cards are currently not being accepted as a form of payment.

If, for whatever reason, you do not have access to a credit or debit card, you can apply for an LNAT voucher, details of which are listed below.

LNAT Voucher

Applicants who do not have access to a credit or debit card can apply for the LNAT voucher. This will enable them to process their application and still submit it online. They will have to send either a cheque, cash, or make a bank transfer in exchange for the electronic voucher, which you can then enter online at the time of booking.

LNAT Bursary

In some circumstances, candidates may be eligible to apply for the LNAT bursary. This scheme is available to candidates who are having difficulty in paying for their assessment. Candidates who wish to apply for the LNAT bursary, must do so prior booking their test.

Be prepared for the bursary to take at least a week to process, and therefore applicants should consider this when planning their application in relation to the deadline.

PREPARING
FOR THE
LNAT

HINTS AND TIPS

No one can teach you the LNAT. Unlike many other tests you will have sat previously, this test does not require strong levels of intellectual ability. Yes, the test is tough, and yes, it is used in a competitive selection process, but the aim of the LNAT is primarily to determine *'able'* candidates, who illustrate the skills and mind-set needed as a potential law student.

A good way to prepare for the LNAT is to understand the expectations and requirements to improve your chances of overall success.

<u>Before your LNAT:</u>

- Ensure that you register online as soon as possible, to make sure that you receive the date and venue of your choice;

- Make sure that you research the deadlines and important dates associated with your chosen institution. Remember, every university has different LNAT deadlines, so it is your responsibility to find out when they are;

- After creating your online account, make sure that you update your profile with any changes, to guarantee your acceptance for the LNAT;

- Your personal identification documents need to match the details found on your online account. Any discrepancies will result in your inability to sit the test;

- Payment needs to be made at the same time of booking your slot. Be sure to have a valid credit or debit card at hand;

- You may be entitled to an LNAT bursary. Research prior to making your booking to see if you are eligible for any financial support;

- Bring your photographic identification and the printed confirmation email with you on the day of your assessment. Without it, you will be unable to sit the test;

- Improve your scores by engaging in issues surrounding current affairs, both locally and internationally;

- Read quality newspapers to ensure that you improve your knowledge on social, political, financial and technological matters.

MULTIPLE-CHOICE QUESTION TIPS:

- You have 42 questions to answer in the time frame of 1 hour and 35 minutes. You need to make sure that you distribute your time wisely;

- Aim for an equal amount of time per question. You will find some questions easier than others, which means that you can spend less time on the questions you find easier. Finding the right balance is crucial;

- Reading the passage is extremely important. Read the passage through carefully in order to gain a complete understanding of the concepts, tone of voice, position that the author holds, the argument being made, etc;

- Only one answer is correct. Whilst some answer choices may seem relatively similar, the questions are designed by a *'matter of degree'*. Thus, you need to work out the ambiguities of each wrong answer, in order to work out which of the options is the correct answer;

- There are no trick questions; the test is merely designed to assess your ability to eliminate the wrong answers by working out the discrepancies. Pay attention to what words are used, this may change which answer option is correct;

- You will receive a mark for each correct answer, no marks are deducted for incorrect answers. So, if you really are struggling to work out the correct answer, eliminate the answers that you know to be incorrect, and take a guess out of the remaining answers;

- You can skip a multiple-choice question and come back to it by marking them for 'review'. You will need to go back to the question *before* you finish the multiple-choice section. **You will not be able to go back to the multiple-choice questions once you begin the essay section.**

ESSAY QUESTION TIPS:

- For this section, you will have 40 minutes in which to answer **one** question from a choice of three possible essay topics;

- Planning your answer and working through a mental structure of what to include in your answer will help in terms of time management. If you make a solid plan before you begin writing, chances are you will have a better understanding of what you want to include in your essay;

- Generally, the essay section should be between 500-600 words;

- You should aim to spend the first 15 minutes of your time planning and writing your introduction. Spending this much time on this part of your essay will demonstrate to the reader that you have carefully thought about what you want to say;

- You should spend 15 minutes on the main body of your essay. This will include all of the main points and arguments that you wish to make. Do not waffle. Provide evidence and examples to support your reasoning and hypothesis, in a clear and concise manner;

- You need to think realistically about how much time you have to make the number of points you want to discuss. Distributing your time between each point will not only make your essay read more coherently, but it will ultimately demonstrate to the reader that you have good time management skills;

- You should spend the remaining 10 minutes concluding and re-reading your essay. Your conclusions should only focus on the points that you have already referred to. Summarise your key points and demonstrate your view/opinion on the overall matter;

- The essay does not want you to 'sit on the fence' with your answers. You need to take a side and make a compelling argument.

TIME MANAGEMENT

Multiple-Choice Questions	Essay Question
You already know that for this section, you will have 42 questions to answer in 1 hour and 35 minutes.	You will have 40 minutes in which to complete one essay question.

Multiple-Choice Questions

You already know that for this section, you will have 42 questions to answer in 1 hour and 35 minutes.

- That means, on average, you need to spend approximately 2 minutes and 20 seconds per question. (This is without reading the passage!);

- Depending on your strengths and weaknesses, some questions will be considerably harder than others, and so will require more time. However, if you really are struggling, don't obsess about that question. Move onto the next and go back to it at the end, if you have time;

- Reading the passage requires a great deal of attention. Reading the passage once carefully and gaining an overall understanding will save time when it comes to answering the questions;

- After reading each question, you should know roughly where it is being discussed in context of the passage, which will save valuable time;

- If you really struggle with a particular question, you can leave it for 'review' and come back to it before you begin the essay section;

- The more you practice reading and thinking, the more effective you will become at answering the multiple-choice questions;

Essay Question

You will have 40 minutes in which to complete one essay question.

- Use the first 15 minutes to plan and write your introduction. You should have a basic understanding of the key points you want to make, the conclusion you hope to reach, and a general understanding of how you want your essay to read;

- The next 15 minutes should be used for the main body of your essay. Include the main points you want to make; and divide your time up equally in order to write a sufficient amount for each point;

- You will receive more marks for fewer points, but stronger detail and analysis; as opposed to cramming in brief points and not explaining them in enough detail;

- The last 10 minutes should focus on summarising your argument. Do not introduce any new points, and make sure that you have supported your argument with a conclusion that is effective and persuasive;

- It is often said that, if a person were to read an introduction and a conclusion, they should have a general understanding of what would be included in the main body of the essay;

Multiple-Choice Questions	Essay Question
• Try to keep track of time as you work through the multiple-choice section. Don't rush through your answers, but remember not to spend too long on one question; • Read newspapers and articles regarding current affairs. Reading and thinking logically in terms of culture and economy will undoubtedly increase your performance for the multiple-choice questions.	• Be straightforward and to the point with your writing style and argument. Make clear and concise points and support them where possible; • Practice writing essay topics regarding current affairs. Read newspapers to expand your wider knowledge on contemporary issues.

READING AND CRITICAL THINKING

The LNAT requires a great deal of attention in regards to reading comprehension and critically analysing information. The test is not a knowledge test. Instead, it focuses on the key skills and qualities that are essential for anyone who wishes to be successful on an undergraduate law degree programme.

The LNAT is extremely difficult because it is hard to revise for. The best preparation for a test like this is to practice sample papers, testing questions and improve the key skills and qualities being assessed. Becoming familiar will undoubtedly better your overall performance.

Reading

You can prepare for the LNAT by undertaking lots of reading. Reading quality newspapers will allow you to think critically in regards to:

• Issues being addressed;
• The assumptions being made;
• Information that is relied upon in order to reach a conclusion;
• The position of the author;
• What the main argument is;
• Thinking of counter-arguments to challenge the argument.

As mentioned above, we advise that you spend some time reading quality newspapers.

Listed below are some of the newspapers that are worth reading:

The Economist	The Financial Times	The Guardian
The Independent	The NY Times	The Times
The Daily Telegraph	The Washington Post	The Irish Times

SAMPLE
MULTIPLE-CHOICE
QUESTIONS

SECTION A OF THE LNAT

Erotic Novels

A The notion of erotica and fantasy has sparked a huge feminist furore over women being submissive and adhering to a male-domineering hierarchy. Within British society, we as feminists and strong believers of equality, find it difficult to accept erotic novels as anything more than an enticement for women to become trapped in a world full of male egos and demeaning ideas of femininity and sexuality.

B I am no stranger to the bestsellers of erotic fiction; books based upon pure lust, sexual desire and power. I find myself quite engrossed, yet also extremely discontented. Stories centre on young male figures, who ooze power and authority. These men seek a woman who shows willingness to surrender in sexual encounters. To me, this depicts an out-dated portrayal of relationships, and yet I continue to read them. Why? It's simple. It's a different way of looking at romance, which combines passion with erotica and stimulation, something we subliminally yearn.

C One of the bestsellers in erotic fiction draws upon a mixture of romance, passion, power, lust and fantasy. One of the biggest themes of current feminist beliefs, is to champion the idea that a woman's body is her own possession, and what she does with it is up to her. It is a consensual feeling for feminists to believe power is being wrestled from us. However, by buying into these fictional concepts of love, passion and relationships, we surrender our freedom and our body.

D Erotic fiction perpetuates absurd, outdated and overrated psychosexual rituals which make society more tangled and indulged in the distorted views of erotica. Erotic fiction is a 'call-out' for the next generation to fixate themselves with. Is this what a hundred years of woman's movement and gaining equal opportunities has prepared us for? The rallying cry of the educated 21st female on ideas of sexuality and empowerment?

Question 1. Which of the authors infers, but does not state, their ideas on a degrading ideology of women?

A – Authors A and B.

B – Authors B and D.

C – Author D.

D – Authors B and C.

E - All of them.

Answer

Question 2. In author C's paragraph, the term "champion" is used to...

A – Support the claim of a woman's body is her own possession.

B – Reject the claim that a woman's body is her own possession.

C – Challenge the claim that a woman is in charge of her own body.

D – Challenge the feminist perspective of the female body.

E – Support the claims of feminists regarding the female body.

Answer

Question 3. Which of the following is *not* used by the writers, to express their strong views against domination?

A – It has taken years for women to gain social status.

B – Equality needs to be maintained within society.

C – Sexual empowerment is hard to overcome.

D – Men believe that they are superior to the female body.

E – Woman are in a position of confinement, inflicted by the male power of society.

Answer

HOW TO ANSWER THE QUESTIONS

Within the multiple-choice section of the exam, you will be provided with different styles of question, in order to assess your ability to analyse comprehension. It is important that you understand the skills that are being tested in this section and how they are extremely specific and tailored to aspiring law students.

The three main types of questions that you can expect to answer during the multiple-choice section are as follows:

- Argument Questions;
- Literary Style Questions;
- Analytical Questions.

In order for you to work out these types of question, you need to have a strong understanding of what they refer to. The following pages will look at these questions in further detail, to give you a clearer understanding of what is involved in part 1 of the LNAT.

Argument Questions

The passages that you will be presented with will be structured in some form of an argument. Whether that be one argument written by one writer, or multiple arguments written by several writers. You will need to be able to recognise what the writer/s is arguing, and the position that they take in regards to the topic being discussed.

These types of questions primarily assess your ability to understand arguments. The questions are usually broken down into phrases such as:

> 'The main argument the author is trying to make is...'

Or

> 'The writer is arguing that...'

Both of these are types of *positive* phrases used to indicate what the author is trying to argue.

Negative phrases are used to highlight what the author is not arguing. These may include:

> *'The writer does not argue that...'*

Or

> *'The writer does not claim that...'*

Sometimes, you may be required to assess the strength of an argument. Being able to distinguish between strong and weak arguments is a vital skill for any aspiring law student. You need to be able to recognise the importance of claims being made, and whether or not these views can be challenged.

You may be given questions in the style of:

> *'Which of the following bests highlights the main argument...'*

Or

> *'Which of the following can be assumed based on the main argument...'*

No matter what style of question you are given, understanding the passage is extremely important. If you are able to work out what the author is trying to say, and what claims and/or assumptions are being stated, it will allow you to have a clear vision of the overall argument.

Literary Style Questions

These types of question refer to types of expressions and how well the author articulates themselves. Literary style questions will test your understanding of the argument by questioning the contextual meanings of words, phrases, punctuation and tones which have been expressed, usually for a particular reason.

Primarily, these types of questions focus on meaning and intent. Questions may appear as followed:

> *'Which of the following phrases is used to illustrate...'*

Or

> *'The writer uses the word _ _ _ _ _ _ to suggest...'*

Language is an important part of the legal sector. You need to be able to articulate and appreciate underlying meanings that can often be abstract, obsolete, indifferent or obscure. A key thing to remember is to look at the meaning on its own, as well as reading it in relation to the overall argument.

Analytical Questions

Analytical questions rely heavily on interpretation. They focus on what may follow after, or even prior, to the argument. These types of questions look at the wider framework in which the passage may have been written, and how this could influence the writer's arguments.

Questions regarding analysis could be seen as followed:

'Which of the following is implied, but not stated...'

Or

'What can be assumed from...'

In order to work out these types of question, it is important that a) you have a clear understanding of the argument and the point that the author is trying to make, and b) you think about *consistency*, and what can be related to the ideas and claims which remain *consistent* throughout the passage.

The Multiple-Choice Section

Overall, the multiple-choice section of the LNAT is purely intended to test a set of particular skills required for law students. Read the passages carefully and understand what each question is asking you, before attempting to answer. Note, these questions are not designed to trick you. The answer can be found in the extract, if you have read it properly and understood the author's argument.

SAMPLE QUESTION – ANSWERS

For the sample question above, *'Erotic Novels'*, we have provided detailed answers and explanations to show what answer is correct, and the reasons why.

Question 1. Which of the authors infers, but does not state, their ideas on a degrading ideology of women?

Answer = D. Author D does not state their ideas on a degrading ideology of women. All of the other authors give examples and explanations as women being degraded in erotic fiction, whereas author D only implies this in their argument, it is not actually stated.

Question 2. In paragraph C, the term "champion" is used to…

Answer = A. The correct answer for this question is answer option A. The use of the word "champion" is used to support the claim that a woman's body is her own possession. The word "champion" is used in aid of support, and this answer provides a clear and concise argument in relation to the context of the passage.

Question 3. Which of the following is *not* used by the writers to express their strong views against domination?

Answer = D. Each writer expresses several views in regards to 'erotic' fiction and the female body. The correct answer for this question is answer D: 'that men believe they are superior to the female body'. In nowhere in the passage does any of the writers mention the beliefs of an actual man. The writers only indicate the dominance and power which men hold over women, but under no circumstances do they mention male views on submissive behaviour or male dominance.

MULTIPLE-CHOICE
(SECTION 1)

You have 95 minutes in which to read the 12 passages and answer all 42 questions.

1. The Prominence of Fernand Braudel

French historian and author Fernand Braudel, became one of the most significant historians of the 20th century. As the leader of the post-World War II Annales School, Braudel made several key contributions to historical theory and research.

Despite theorists Febrve and Bloch being the initial founders of the Annales School, Braudel was one of the first historians to gain widespread support for his theories. Braudel's theory suggested that history should create data from the use of social sciences, in order to provide a more accurate and historical view of human society.

Under Braudel's influence and direction, the Annales School acquired global recognition in promoting new theories of history. It subsequently synthesised life as we know it. With politics and war effecting areas such as the economy, communication, transportation, agriculture, technology and citizenship; history was constantly being made, moulded and manipulated.

The Annales School challenged initial reductionism of the Marxist view on structuralism. It aimed for a "total history" that centred on theorising human experiences in relation to culture, events and the environment. Braudel made initial conceptions regarding three main temporalities that played a vital role in determining history. The *evenementielle* referred to the subject of history, comprising of short-lived events that play a crucial part in historical debate. These often included battles, revolutions and actions which changed the history of society. The *longue duree*, a wave of great time and length which focuses on environmental factors; was a concept that Braudel found most fascinating. Braudel also focussed on the importance of the link between economics, time and culture.

The *longue duree* focuses on everyday aspects which build up an idea of what people eat, what they wear, what they say, and how they travel; all of which is built into a 'grounded structure' that defines the social world. This concept not only extended the idea of time, but historical space. When time spans are considered on a larger scale, geography begins to take a role. Braudel's thesis and doctorate regarding the Mediterranean during Phillip II's reign, explored geography as an external "structure" that infiltrated human life.

However, Braudel's work has been challenged and faulted for his imprecisions within the approach of theory analysis. Braudel's work minimises the differences between social sciences and therefore provides no clear or solid structure. His detailed thesis into the realms of relevant historical phenomena makes it difficult to define or examine the boundaries of observation. Yet, many studies that use Braudel's theories and analysis, ask significant and probing questions which traditional theorists were considered to overlook.

Question 1

The primary purpose of the author's work is...

A – To outline the influences of Braudel's works, and discuss the differences of traditional theories.

B – To illustrate Braudel's contemporary concepts in relation to social science.

C – To highlight the importance of Braudel's work in attempt to dismiss the views of traditional theorists.

D – To demonstrate the depths to which Braudel's work centres on *longue duree.*

E – To challenge other theorists work in relation to historical concepts and prove Braudel's hypothesis as an accurate account of history.

Answer

Question 2

In the passage, the author does not...

A – Examine a range of aspects of human activity.

B – Visualise history in a range of different time scales.

C – Promote new forms of historical thesis.

D – Point out the link between the increase in liberation and economics.

E – Challenge traditional methods of historical debate.

Answer

Question 3

The reason the author refers to Febrve and Bloch, is to...

A – Challenge the views of Braudel's concept of economics.

B – Demonstrate that Braudel's work is flawed with limitations in regards to historical observations.

C – Highlight the importance of social theory in relation to economics.

D – Strengthen the traditional theories on the subjects of economics and society.

E – Highlight initial assumptions made regarding Braudel's work on economics.

Answer

Question 4

The use of the word "synthesised" in context of the passage, *mostly* suggests...

A – Social sciences play an important role in forming historical observation.

B – History should be preserved by the social aspects of our world.

C – History needs to be produced by focusing on the social sciences.

D – Social sciences is the only way in which history can be created.

E – Economics are a vital part of the historical knowledge we assume to be the truth.

Answer

2. The Distorted Views of the Media

The myriad landscape of the media infiltrates every inch of the social world, and can be accessed almost anywhere, by anyone. The media has changed considerably over the years, from information reported through newspapers and television, to a world that is transfixed with the realms of online access. It highlights the major growths in how the world communicates, and how these modes of communication have changed considerably over time.

How then, can we be sure to trust the channels which present to us a single form of interpretation? What is the quality of the information that we are receiving? Does the media focus on quantity more than assuring quality? Ultimately, it is not so much about where the information comes from, but the extent to which these mediums produce reliable and partial accounts of news.

The media has become somewhat slanted in recent years. No matter what the medium, the information that they create and produce can be, and is often challenged. Criticisms in regards to fabrication, distortion, manipulation and interpretation, suggests that publishers and distributors are more concerned with maintaining and accumulating circulation figures, as opposed to being centred on truth, justice and value.

The fabrication of beauty and body image is a major issue that is often portrayed within an array of media formats. It continues to stir debate regarding how such images carry inaccurate and biased accounts of the truth, particularly in regards to women. For years, the media have shown visual ideas of the "ideal image" of what a "perfect woman" should look like. Magazines, films and commercials are constantly *spoon-feeding* girls and women with the idea that they can only achieve beauty if they have long legs, toned muscles and curves in all of the right places. Although the media continues to boast about this "sparkling" image of what they deem to be beautiful, to most of us, it is an alien concept that we simply cannot live up to.

The pressures to conform to this ideal image sully our everyday lives. Do I look fat? Does my hair look great? Do I have a great complexion? These are all typical questions that the majority of young girls and women find themselves asking every day. Why then, does the media continue to distort this superficial image that is unattainable by the majority? Tabloid newspapers are often criticised for their portrayal of a woman's body image. Women are a controversial issue within feminist debate and media representations. Women are demoralised and represented as "sex objects", in order to produce a visual aid for the male gaze.

Conveying women in this supposedly "ideal image", is no different than conveying every man to be "macho". The media represent men in a particular way that represents ideas of *what it takes to be a real man*. Most media portrayals focus on heterosexual, white males who are physically attractive, with bulging biceps, killer abs, and show strong independence and financial success. When will media images convey something with more truth and realism, to which their audiences can relate?

Question 5

Within the third paragraph, the writer *assumes* that...

A – Newspapers are the foundation of distorted imagery.

B – Publishers of newspapers are the people who decide what gets printed in their paper.

C – Newspapers continue to adopt a writing style that is based on bias and controversy.

D – Distorted imagery cannot be avoided.

E – The media are responsible for the social issues in which girls face regarding body image.

Answer

Question 6

In paragraph five, the writer uses what literary technique, to demonstrate the link between distorted imagery and body image?

A – Simile.

B – Metaphor.

C – Irony.

D – Personification.

E – Analogy.

Answer

Question 7

The writer puts inverted commas around "ideal image" and "perfect woman" because...

A – He is dismissing them.
B – They are quotations.
C – He wants to draw attention to them.
D – They are used in a superficial way.
E – He doesn't think they reflect true beauty.

Answer

Question 8

The author compares women's "ideal image" with the notions of "what it takes to be a real man" because...

A – It adheres to the common representations in which media has inflicted upon society.
B – The media needs to be challenged in regards to stereotypical representations.
C – It demonstrates the influences of the media and how this impacts society.
D – It highlights how women and men adhere to these stereotypes represented in the media.
E – The media are the only means of conveying an image of what people can admire to.

Answer

3. Television Ads vs. Internet Ads

A study in 2009 conducted by the IAB, showed that a record figure of over £1 billion had been spent on web ads, making the UK the first major economy to spend more on internet advertising than television advertising.

Marketing strategies in television maintain a stable advertising medium. Television continues to use strategies similar to those used from several years ago. They continue to advertise products using actors and a narrative that usually lasts between 30 to 60 seconds. However, recent technological changes and advances have imposed upon the world of television. The internet is a global phenomenon that has been subject to dynamic changes, particularly in advertising and marketing. This forces other mediums such as television to evolve and adapt their strategies in order to remain in business.

With the internet now accounting for over 23% of all advertising money, it has taken just over a decade to surpass the leading marketing medium for over half a century. It has outshined television through its advanced strategic procedures and strategies, which undoubtedly illustrates the impact on television as an advertising medium. However, many advertisers are reluctant to make this shift from television advertising to the internet, because they still see television as the main form of marketing. They believe that television appeals to a wider, mass audience which does not exclude the older generation, who are less familiar with internet devices.

Taking into consideration pre-existing brand knowledge, it is imperative to obtain valid comparisons regarding different media platforms. It can be argued that the internet attracts consumers who contain lower levels of pre-existing brand knowledge, whereas television advertising offers higher levels of product knowledge. The need to consider these "initial conditions" is a significant part of determining how well the marketing strategy for each medium is working, and evaluate the long-term repercussions that will eventually affect the medium as a marketing distributor.

The rise of internet marketing continues to develop, and as time goes on, it is more than likely that we will be reliant on such technological advances. Online advertisers use marketing strategies such as banners, pop-up ads and social networking, to attract potential and existing customers. These methods ensure companies of low costing marketing strategies, which build up large audiences and generate sufficient numbers of sales. Despite some customers failing to see the positives of these adverts, instead finding them to be intrusive and annoying, companies are investing more time, money and effort in the hopes of "capturing a market stake" in the burgeoning online economy.

Our society has become fixated with the internet, and it continues to manifest in our everyday lives. Is online advertising more advantageous compared to other mediums? Are television adverts dying-out? Can online and television compete with each other in a society that faces huge technological change?

Question 9

According to the passage, the author clearly indicates that the *main* way in which television and internet advertising differ, is through...

A – The cost of introducing new strategies to the medium.
B – The drawbacks of traditional mediums of advertising.
C – The 'dying out' of the need for advertisements.
D – The pace at which the two mediums evolve.
E – The audience which is reached by the different mediums.

Answer

Question 10

The term "burgeoning" in the phrase, "capturing a market stake" in a burgeoning online economy, is used to...

A – Illustrate the decline in television marketing.
B – Convey the importance of marketing strategies.
C – Challenge other media platforms in relation to profit.
D – Highlight the growth and influences of online marketing.
E – Identify the common strategies used amongst online advertisers.

Answer

Question 11

The use of the evidence claiming that "the internet [is] now accounting for over 23% of all advertising money" is used to illustrate how television…

A – Is not making any money.
B – Is no longer in demand.
C – Continues to remain as the leading marketing platform.
D – Has completely 'died out'.
E – Is no longer the leading advertising platform.

Answer

4. The Threats of Social Networking

Social networking has unquestionably become a global phenomenon, which I believe is having a huge affect on our social world. Social networking sites such as Facebook, MySpace and Twitter have experienced exponential growth during the 21st century, and yet some users remain oblivious to how much their social networking profiles can shape, influence and affect their everyday lives.

Information that is posted on these sites is likely to come back and haunt a person in the future. Just think of a social networking site as a type of "global database". You are posting information, facts about yourself, images etc, into your very own "database"; acting as a log of your personal behaviour for others to view. This is a great concern for many parents, who feel obliged to check how secure their child is whilst they're online.

An example of the impact of social networking occurred in America, where students were faced with court charges for underage drinking, a situation that had it not been shared on their social networking profiles, would never have been known otherwise. The students in question were unaware of the impact of their behaviour when posting the evidence online.

Furthermore, employers often use these sites as a way of maintaining access to their employees outside of the working environment. Although this can be considered morally wrong, employers can track your profile in order to find controversial issues, sensitive matters or inappropriate misconduct. They do this in order to determine the professionalism of their employees outside of the working environment, and to determine their 'suitability' in relation to their careers. Employers can also use social networking as a type of 'screening process', before employing a potential employee. They are able to conduct background checks on an individual before they meet in person. Our rights are constantly supressed by this insane notion of living through social networking sites.

Not only are social networking sites being 'checked' by employers, they are also becoming an increasing concern in terms of bullying, grooming and abuse. With a small minority of users actually utilising the security system to its fullest, profiles are subsequently left open to everyone. A profile can be used to track someone down, find out what they are up to, stalk an individual, and become somewhat obsessive over the lives of other people.

Although more and more people are becoming aware of online security, many regular users still fail to secure their profile in order to protect themselves from external harm. Ensuring security settings are filtered, so only people you know can access the contents of your profile, will help prevent any harm. Searching for any harmful information regarding yourself that you or somebody else has posted and removing it from your profile, will decrease your chances of being accused of anything by employers, parents or others. Making sure to never post anything on these sites that could be considered as highly offensive, discriminatory, unprofessional or inappropriate, will make sure that you are being 'safe' whilst being online.

Question 12

Which of the following would *best* describe the relationship of the last paragraph, with the rest of the passage?

A – Offers examples in regards to previous assertions mentioned in the passage.

B – It summarises the overall argument.

C – It offers a counter-argument against the points made previously in the passage.

D – It provides suggestions to improve the issues as previously stated.

E – It generates possible consequences of the issues as previously claimed.

Answer

Question 13

Which of the following *best* describes the author's tone in regards to his attitude about social networking sites?

A – Strongly pessimistic.

B – Discouraged.

C – Guarded.

D – Upset.

E – Highly optimistic.

Answer

Question 14

All of the following are indicated as possible threats in relation to social networking, *except...*

A – Police involvement concerning unsuitable behaviour.

B – Parents acting as a concerned individual in regards to the actions of their children.

C – Future employers who hope to evaluate a candidate prior to meeting them.

D – Schools, colleges and universities expressing concerns regarding their students and their behaviour.

E – Unwanted attention from people who use these sites as a way or luring vulnerable users into a false sense of security.

Answer

Question 15

From the passage, the author *implies*, but does not state, that...

A – Information online, once secured, poses no risk of substantial harm.

B – Parents should be stricter regarding their child using the internet.

C – Employers should be allowed to use social networking sites as a means of keeping an eye on existing or future employees.

D – Children are responsible for using the internet safely and securely.

E – Information founded online can be used as evidence in court.

Answer

5. Global Warming

Global warming is already having an impact on our community, and without taking action, the issue will continue to become more of a concern and will affect the future of our world.

Global warming doesn't just mean that the weather will get somewhat warmer. As the planet begins to heat, climate patterns will fluctuate. This will result in extreme and unpredictable weather conditions. While some countries may experience extreme heat, others will experience torrential rain and plummeting temperatures. This is a direct consequence of the way in which the planet has been treated.

Climate change is simply a result of human action. Burning fossil fuels is a clear example of how, over the past 15 decades, the world has become more industrialised and changed the balance of the carbon cycle. Burning fossil fuels such as oil, gas and coal converts carbon into carbon dioxide, and unless it is captured, the carbon dioxide is released into the atmosphere. This climate change is characterised by higher than average global temperatures and increased sea levels.

Not only does fossil fuel contribute to global warming, but breeding cattle is another contributing factor. Within our industrialised society, nations have bred vast numbers of methane-producing animal stock. A moose, for example, contributes massively to global warming, expelling methane of approximately 2,100kg of carbon dioxide emissions, similar to the impact of driving for 8,000 miles.

Forests have a huge role to play in fighting climate change. Forests can be used to absorb and store carbon in their soil and trees. Yet, we continue to cut these forests down with no consideration of the consequences that follow. Why? Why do we continue these actions if we know what the outcome and consequences are going to be? If these forests are frequently being cut down, then all of the stored emissions from the trees will be released into the atmosphere. Up to one fifth of greenhouse gas emissions comes from deforestation and forest degradation, which indicates the scale of the issue and the impact that it causes in terms of global warming.

Some people consider global warming as "natural", yet it is apparent that we, as the central contributors to climate change, need to change our behaviour. Science tells us that although the Earth's climate has always changed; our actions in the way we have treated our planet, remain the most damaging.

Climate change, if not acted upon, will continue to have gross consequences, which will lead to extreme weather conditions, potential rises in sea level, decreased ice environments, and even possible extinction of plants and animals. Ultimately, it will change the world as we know it.

Question 16

According to the passage, the writer *infers*, but does not state, that…

A – Climate change cannot be helped.

B – We need to reduce our own carbon footprint.

C – Climate change is a direct effect of man-made phenomena.

D – We need to maintain a stable environment for all living species.

E – We need to be able to adapt and cope with the constant changes of climate change.

Answer

Question 17

The word "natural" is written with inverted commas, to suggest…

A – The importance of the word "natural" in regards to our natural surroundings.

B – That the writer wanted its readers to pay particular attention to the sentence.

C – The counter-argument that global warming cannot be acted upon.

D – That the writer does not believe global warming to be of natural causes.

E – That the writer does not want its readers to think global warming is acceptable.

Answer

Question 18

From the passage, the writer *infers*, but does not state, that...

A – Global warming is on the increase.

B – The Government needs to become more involved with improving climate change.

C – Deforestation will be a direct cause of dramatic climate change.

D – Ecosystems will be lost or effected due to the sudden changes of climate change.

E – We do not show enough consideration and care towards our environment and social surroundings.

Answer

6. The 9/11 Terrorist Attack

September 11, 2001 is one of the most historically archived events in global history. It was a devastating day, which saw a series of attacks held on four commercial passenger planes flying out from the east coast of the United States. The impact of these attacks was felt around the world, and ultimately changed society forever.

On the morning of September 11th, 19 hijackers took control of four planes; with the intention of causing a catastrophic historical event. Two of the hijacked planes were deliberately crashed into the Twin Towers of the World Trade Centre in New York; the third plane was flown into the Pentagon, Virginia, and the fourth plane never reached its supposed target. It is believed that the passengers and crew members of the fourth plane fought the hijackers, and took back control of the plane. However, despite their best efforts, they were unable to steer out of danger. The plane was targeted to hit Washington D.C, but instead crashed into a field in Pennsylvania.

The Twin Towers are considered a "symbol" of American history, and the site now attracts over 70,000 tourists. America continues to uphold one of the greatest emblems in global history, and faces the future with sheer remarkability, strength and the determination to remain undefeated.

The attack on the United States was described as an evil, despicable, disgusting and violent act of terrorism. The event brought about significant changes in regards to attitudes and concerns about safety and vigilance. These changes have led to a rippling effect that has not only affected the United States, but equally affected the entire welfare of the global economy.

With the total loss of the 9/11 terrorist attack being approximately 3,000 civilians, it was claimed as being the worst loss of life due to terrorism on US soil. The following days and months saw a whole new side of America. What was once considered a country centred on freedom, power and beauty, was now host to one of the most catastrophic events in history.

The manifestation of such an event caused significant political, economical and social disputes. Global relationships would never be the same again. Increased security, bigger safety concerns, and an amplified fear of terrorism, are a direct result of the 9/11 terrorist attacks.

We now live in a world full of anxiety, panic and tragedy that continues to blind our conceptions of contemporary society. We live in constant fear that terrorist attacks will become inevitable, unpredictable and more frequent. We live in a world that is continuously bombarded with threats, risks and uncertainties that make it difficult to forget about the past, and subsequently affect how we handle the present, and how we view the future.

Question 19

According to the passage, the use of the word 'symbolic', in relation to the twin towers, is used by the author to *mainly* identify America as upholding…

A – Beauty and Grace.
B – Power and Influence.
C – Freedom and Beauty.
D – Determined and Fearless.
E – Strength and Indifference.

Answer

Question 20

From the passage, you could *assume* that…

A – The attacks were conducted under a revolutionary act that placed America at the forefront for its attacks.
B – No scientific evidence can be made between the hijackers and political enforcements.
C – The Government had no strong security procedures in place to prevent such attacks.
D – The Government had no control over the safeguarding of the four planes that were hijacked and flown into disaster.
E – The fourth plane, which was aimed at Washington but crashed in Pennsylvania, would have heavily increased the number of fatalities on the day.

Answer

Question 21

The last paragraph is written in conjunction with the rest of the passage, to demonstrate the author's...

A – Response regarding the impact of terrorism for American citizens.

B – Conception of terrorism in relation to political enforcements of Government intervention.

C – Attitudes regarding the significant consequences of an attack that ultimately affected the world forever.

D – Concerns for America's powerful status in regards to influence, freedom and fortitude.

E – Assumptions that global terrorism should be feared and therefore societies need to implement and prepare for action.

Answer

7. The Reign of Henry VIII

English history has witnessed many changes in regards to Kings, Queens, traditions, politics, wealth, status and power. Without this history, we would find it difficult to determine our English culture.

A particularly influential time within English history was during the Reign of Henry VIII. A conceited, manipulative, assertive and downright power-driven man, Henry became King of England in 1509, following the death of his father and eldest brother.

As the author of the book *Assertio Septem*, which attacked Martin Luther and conversely supported the Roman Catholic Church, Henry VIII was conferred by the Pope, in recognition of his work. He was given the title Defender of the Faith. In 1515, Henry VIII introduced Thomas Wolsey as Lord Chancellor. From this, Thomas Wolsey became a significant influence in British history. As one of the most powerful ministers in history, he exercised his services through judicial appointments. Hampton Court Palace, which served as the residence of both Wolsey and Henry at different points in their lives, highlights the status of the ruling class at the time.

Henry VIII is also known to have taken a keen interest in the Royal Navy. Known as the "father of the Royal Navy", when he first became King, there were no more than 5 warships. By the time he died, he had built up around 50 warships and refitted several vessels with the latest gun technology, including the Mary Rose ship.

Henry VIII gained great pleasure from his royal status. Wealth, power and leadership were extremely significant to the lifestyle which he led, and he was acutely aware of what was at stake. He knew the significance of securing a male heir during his reign of England, in order to continue his family name. Henry made it his aim to secure a wife in the hopes of gaining a male son.

The Tudor dynasty in which Henry VIII lived, was established in 1485 and had only seen two monarchs. England, at this time, had not been ruled by a Queen, and the dynasty was not secure in handing the crown to a woman. The risk of allowing a woman to rule disputes, succession or domination of foreign powers through matrimony, was incongruous.

Often taught in schools, Henry VIII is remembered as the man with six wives. In order of marriage, they were: Catherine of Aragon, Anne Boleyn, Jane Seymour, Anne of Cleves, Kathryn Howard and Kathryn Parr. Children in schools are often taught a rhyme in order to remember how Henry VIII's wives died: 'divorced, beheaded, died, divorced, beheaded, survived'.

When Henry VIII became King, the country was Catholic and controlled by the Pope in Rome. When the Pope refused to let him get divorced from his first wife, Henry VIII made himself the head of the Church of England, and granted himself his divorce.

In the later years of Henry's reign, he passed constitution on two issues which ultimately changed the future of English history and the monarchy. These were the Act of Succession, and the Protestant Reformation, which subsequently led to the Church of England.

Question 22

In literary terms, the Hampton Court Palace is used in association with Henry VIII and Thomas Wolsey, to demonstrate...

A – Metaphor.
B – Symbolism.
C – Analogy.
D – Simile.
E – Personification.

Answer

Question 23

From the passage, you could *infer* that the term "Defender of the Faith"...

A – Highlights a person who stands by religious attributes.
B – Pinpoints the importance of the Pope in relation to faith and religion.
C – Highlights the discrepancies between Martin Luther and Henry VIII.
D – Demonstrates the sovereign of England.
E – Demonstrates the sovereign of religion.

Answer

Question 24

From the passage, we can *assume* that Protestant Reformation...

A – Aimed to provide retribution for people who went against the reformation.

B – Is a rebellion against prior traditions led by Martin Luther.

C – Marked the end of the reign for Henry VIII.

D – Marked the new beginning of Henry VIII being crowned King of England.

E – Aimed to reform the beliefs, traditions and practices of the Church.

Answer

Question 25

In the fifth paragraph, the author discusses the importance of Henry VIII securing a male heir, because...

A – He did not bond with the daughters in which were conceived during marriage.

B – Giving the opportunity to women to rule was deemed controversial.

C – His misogynistic ways refuses to let women be responsible for ruling a country.

D – It goes against the male-domineering hierarchy of the time, where women were not seen capable of ruling.

E – He would be seen as a weak ruler by offering the ruling status to a woman.

Answer

8. String Theory and Scientific Discoveries

We live in a world that is constantly changing. As human beings, we are always making new scientific discoveries, and producing theories, contemplations and ideas on how we began our existence. One of these theories is string theory.

In an attempt to explain all of the fundamentals of nature, superstring theory analyses the vibrations of tiny supersymmetric strings. For example, let's compare string theory with a guitar in order to gain a clearer understanding of how string theory actually works. A guitar is tuned by the stretching and tweaking of strings, which are put under tension to form vibrations and create sound. The musical note that is played, depends on how that string is plucked, where you position your hands, and how much tension the strings are under. This is very similar to the way in which string theory works.

The strings need to be put under tension in order to create some impact and cause a noticeable outcome. Unlike the strings on a guitar, the strings in string theory are not tied down. They are floating in 'space and time' but are still restrained by tension, and therefore still form vibrations.

String theorists need to devise measures that will allow them to analyse and interpret string theory in order to make their discoveries and experiment with scientific findings.

In my opinion, string theory does not make for a compelling argument. Astro-physicists will automatically conclude that the future of physics can be solely linked to this notion of string theory. String theory is one of those theories that is often hyped-up, like a film in the cinema that has become overrated and over-advertised, but turns out to be a complete failure. There are many logical inconsistencies that can be used to argue against string theory. It is all well and good on paper, but applying that theory into real life application, proves somewhat difficult and uncertain. One of the biggest problems is that the strings in association with string theory are so small that it is practically impossible for theorists to decipher accurate results. Take these experiments with a pinch of salt. String theory is, and will continue to be, a work in progress with questionable results.

The key features of string theory suggest that all objects within our universe are made up of vibrating strings, also known as filaments and membranes of energy. It attempts to reconcile general contingency of gravity with this notion of quantum physics. Theorists also believe that several other, often unobservable dimensions, must exist.

String theory, also known as 'The Theory of Everything' is a unifying theory of physics between quantum physics and gravity, in the hopes of explaining all of the matters and natures of the universe.

Question 26

Which of the following words is *not* used to highlight the negative qualities of string theory?

A – "...unobservable".
B – "...hyped-up".
C – "...a work in progress".
D – "...inconsistencies".
E – "...unifying".

Answer [   ]

Question 27

What is the flaw of the concept of "The Theory of Everything", in which the author *infers*?

A – It presents a limited picture of choices available in order to support the situation.
B – Reasoning assumes a causal connection without good evidence or support.
C – It does not allow for any other possibilities of science.
D – The inference is a sweeping generalisation that relies on some or many or all scientific evidence.
E – It confuses the correlation and cause that forms a *post hoc* account whereby if A happens before B; A causes B.

Answer [   ]

Question 28

The author uses the phrase "pinch of salt", to...

A – Emphasis the scale to which string theory is placed.
B – Highlight the truth underlying the theory of science.
C – Indicate the underlying messages in which string theory offers.
D – Suggest to the reader to understand string theory with considerable doubt and scepticism.
E – Reinforce that there is no scientific evidence to back up the ideas of string theory.

Answer

Question 29

The author compares string theory with a guitar, to...

A – Demonstrate the similarities in string size.
B - Demonstrate the differences of string tension.
C – Explain how the vibrations of a guitar are similar to that in string theory.
D – Highlight the importance of sound in relation to science.
E – Indicate the importance of the strings to produce an outcome.

Answer

9. Propaganda, Power and Persuasion

Propaganda is a form of communication that attempts to achieve a particular response, via persuasive language. Propaganda has been commonly used throughout history and in relation to journalism, politics, science, psychology, sociology and culture.

One of the most famous wartime posters was an image of Lord Kitchener in 1914, pointing towards its viewers. This image was so powerful and persuasive that it was adopted by the USA in both World War I and World War II. What makes for a powerful poster? How does it engage with its audience? Is it morally right to subject people to propaganda messages?

The use of posters in wartime as a propaganda marketing strategy, was a great way for the sender to communicate its message to the public domain. With no television or internet back in World War II, the sender needed to use a means of communication that would effectively reach a mass audience in a time-efficient manner. These posters were used in an array of ways in order to get the point across. The posters focused on conservation and production, secrecy, allegiance, recruitment and home efforts, in hope to form some allegiance between the public and those in power.

The use of propaganda is all around us. Even without knowing it, we are subjects to information, messages and advertisements that are distributed for a particular reason or purpose. Propaganda is like an injection. We are 'injected' and 'filled' with information and ideas, which are regarded as the truth.

Governments have a vast amount of resources to help shape, manipulate and misinform citizens in order to convey a particular message. They use areas such as conflict, protests, education, politics and leadership to spread their message, and subsequently mislead and deceive their targets.

Not only does propaganda control and alter the main balance of power within society, but it hides the fact that organisations and groups use propaganda to win over the public. They do this through substantial orchestrations of appeal, packaged to conceal the fact that their message is based on a persuasive purpose, which often lacks solid supportive reasoning.

Propaganda is a deliberate act that is carefully thought out in terms of the most effective, logical and promising strategies. It is used both deliberately and systematically to highlight the important ideological aspirations which governments use to maintain their position in power. Many people are ignorant to the fact that propaganda is affecting their behaviour and attitudes about a particular situation. As soon as the public become aware that they are part of a propaganda strategy, they will be able to act upon it. They will be able to choose whether to accept it or reject it, rather than following it because of their obliviousness to the fact that they are being manipulated and directed to follow a certain path.

Question 30

Which of the following gives the *best* reason as to why the poster of Lord Kitchener pointed towards its audience?

A – To make it more personal.

B – To attract a mass audience.

C – To make the motives behind the poster questionable.

D – To act as a warning sign.

E – To illustrate a message aimed directly at the public.

Answer

Question 31

In context of the passage, why does the author compare propaganda to "injections"?

A – To show how the public are poisoned with information given by the Government.

B – To demonstrate the public's thinking, without them having to think at all.

C – To demonstrate how important messages are sent to the public.

D – To highlight the persuasive measures used by the Government in order to maintain allegiance with the public.

E – To demonstrate how the public are inserted with information that is manipulated by those in power.

Answer

Question 32

In the last paragraph, the author would *most* likely agree with the assumption that...

A – Propaganda only benefits those in control.

B – The moment people become aware of propaganda, it becomes ineffective.

C – Propaganda is used to serve reasonable purposes.

D – Propaganda is a technique used to create social order.

E – Propaganda relies on unstated assumptions that are communicated to its audience, rather than highlighting the actual purpose.

Answer

10. Creative Pedagogy

Creative pedagogy is a concept that was primarily designed to teach pupils how to learn in a creative and active manner, by allowing them to become creators: creators of themselves, and creators of their future.

Creative pedagogy is a concept that derives from both science and art. A creative learner is someone who is able to demonstrate high levels of problem solving, imaginative thinking and innovative thoughts, all of which are deemed essential qualities in real life.

Theorist Jean Piaget and his works on child development and observation highlight the importance of education. His views on child mind-sets and development, played a huge role in developing his works on educational theory. He conducted his studies through multiple observations, whilst engaging with activities that helped him to gain an understanding of the different processes involved in the developmental stages of children's learning.

He noted that children's thinking did not develop quickly, nor smoothly. It exposed him to the different stages in the development process whereby children would transition into new ways of thinking. These transitions occurred at different stages of a child's learning development. Piaget's work demonstrates the struggle to implement a development strategy that could be used to analyse every child.

Creative pedagogy is proposed to provide a more holistic view of enhancing children's learning skills and ability. It is argued that there are three main areas which need to be addressed in relation to creative pedagogy. Firstly, there is *creative learning*. This deals with the actions of a child. Creative learning focuses primarily on a child's intrinsic curiosity and imagination. Typically, it can be found through the use of drama activities, which allow a child to engage with experiences that incorporate active learning through creative thinking and imagination.

Secondly, *creative teaching* is the stage which focuses mainly on the teaching styles and techniques used by teachers and/or social workers. It is argued that teaching needs to incorporate imaginative, creative and innovative approaches to allow children to become engaged with the topic. Improvisation is a crucial stage of creative teaching as it allows the teacher to conduct a class that is active and spontaneous, and enables them to utilise their existing knowledge and adapt it by 'living in the moment' and actively seeking involvement.

Teaching for creativity is the third element of creative pedagogy, and considers influential environmental supporting factors. The environment needs to be conducive with the different ways of being creative. This will allow for the creative ideas and behaviour that will ultimately allow children to become independent thinkers.

Question 33

Which of the following words or phrases *best* describes a creative learner, in context of the passage?

A – Intellectual thinker.
B – Highly skilled at drawing and painting.
C – Lateral thinker.
D – Selective thinker.
E – Logical and Analytical thinker.

Answer

Question 34

From the author's passage on Jean Piaget and social development, you could *assume* that individual learners differ from each other by...

A – The stages of development.
B – The progression rate at which children develop.
C – The concepts of which children began to understand.
D – Learning techniques being different for each child.
E – The knowledge and understanding a child has about the social world.

Answer

Question 35

The author uses the word *"holistic"* in context of the passage, to...

A – Provide a more grounded knowledge of creative learning and imagination.

B – Provide a direct teaching approach that has little room for variation.

C – Provide a disciplined curriculum designed to address the key skills required for academic learning.

D – Provide a systematic approach that addresses key skills such as academia and knowledge.

E – Demonstrate how children need to be educated to become well-grounded citizens of society.

Answer

Question 36

According to the passage, the overall *aim* of Piaget's work is used to...

A – Assess how quickly a child develops within educational settings.

B – Demonstrate intellectual developments of children in regards to learning and progression.

C – Explain the mechanisms and structures by which children develop using reasoning and hypotheses.

D – Demonstrate the significance of secondary social structures as being an impact on social development.

E – Relate existing theories and apply them to real life applications.

Answer

11. Children Becoming Teenagers

When they are on the verge of becoming a teenager, you will undoubtedly witness an array of changes in your son or daughter. What once was your innocent and beautiful baby, has now reached the stage of adolescence, and must now begin the 'painful' process of developing into a young man or woman.

Now on the cusp of adolescence, you and your child are about to embark on a great voyage. They will be a metamorphosed silhouette of what once was a child. It will be a bumpy ride that is bound to involve tears, laughter, maturity, naivety and independence. You will unwittingly be the guidepost through every experience, as your child blossoms into a young adult.

You will notice at times that everything you do or say to your 'baby' is wrong. I am not going to sugar coat it, but no matter how many children you have, this will never get easier. You should expect to deal with plenty of heated debates, arguments, pleas and tantrums.

As the hormones begin to take over, a teenager will start to experience changes to their body, attitude and behaviour. As a parent, it will be a struggle to remain calm and patient with a child who constantly makes it their aim to drive you up the wall, push you away, and throw all their hissy-fits at you. Stress about exams, making new friends, joining a new school, having their first crush, having their first heartbreak – our teenagers have to deal with a tremendous amount of pressure in order to 'fit' in with the rest of society, and therefore this transition is never easy.

You may experience times when you find yourself looking back over the memories of your teenager, when they were a baby. Now only shadows remain of the child who thought of you as their hero, who followed your every footstep and asked for your words of wisdom and experience. You will find yourself 'losing' your child. Upon adolescence, many teenagers start to become distant, reserved, and independent. They begin to reject the things you say, cancel on your plans, and shut you out; even though all they want is guidance and comfort. This is a difficult process for everyone involved.

When you are being bombarded with tantrums, loud music and disobedience, it can be hard not to take it personally. The fact that we are so close with our children makes it even more painful, and it is not uncommon to feel a certain amount of loneliness when watching your child transform from an innocent and naïve child, into a heated and troubled teenager. However, if you take a step back from the situation, you will see that your troubled teenager needs only sympathy and guidance to spread their wings, and blossom into a beautiful butterfly.

Question 37

In context of the passage, the use of the word "metamorphosed" is used to describe...

A – The transformation from a teenager into an adult.
B – The scientific changes of emotional behaviour.
C – The changes of a human's intellectual behaviour.
D – The transformation and changes from a child into a teenager.
E – The scientific discovery of human nature.

Answer

Question 38

The author uses the phrase, "I am not going to sugar coat it", in order to convey that...

A – You cannot hide the difficulties of raising a teenager.
B – Despite the challenges, parenting is a rewarding feeling.
C – Parenting is a challenging task and should not be taken lightly.
D – Parenting comes with a great deal of responsibility.
E – Teenagers make it their job to be challenging for their parents.

Answer

Question 39

The author uses the phrase, "only shadows remain", to refer to...

A – The distant memories of childhood.

B – The life changes which are faced after having a child.

C – Past memories belonging to the child.

D – The unknown future that lies ahead.

E – Past memories belonging to the parent.

Answer

12. Concealed Weaponry and the Public

The concealed carry law refers to the act that permits a person to carry a weapon in public, as long as it is carried in a 'concealed' and 'discrete' manner. The carry law has proven to be a "hot" topic in the United States, where people often question whether or not it should be legal to carry concealed weaponry.

One of the most commonly cited reasons for carrying weapons, from pro-gun activists, is that people have a right to defend themselves against the government. These people are, quite frankly, deluded. In the unlikely event that the government did decide to turn against its citizens, a handgun would not be much use. The government has tanks, drones, planes and bombs at its disposal. Unless these people would change the law to allow all citizens access to rocket launchers and other heavy weaponry, they will have to reconcile themselves with the uncomfortable truth that a physical resistance against the US government would be virtually impossible.

Equally as ridiculous is the argument that gun control laws violate the second amendment. The second amendment states, 'a well-regulated militia being necessary to the security of the Free State, the right of the people to keep and bear Arms shall not be infringed'. This is all well and good, if you ignore the power of the US military. Do we need a citizen based military, to ensure American sovereignty? This is the 21st century. We're privileged to have such a strong military presence. If you don't agree with this, then you are by default agreeing that gun control laws violate all restrictions, regardless of the circumstances. In which case, we should give incarcerated murderers and criminals the right to carry guns in prison. Happy hunting, boys.

The majority of studies have shown that gun laws reduce violence. Some people argue that it's not guns that kill people, it is people that kill people. That might be true, but people with guns kill more people than they would if they didn't have guns. All over the world people are angry, depressed and lonely. But there aren't mass shootings every few weeks in England, Spain, Portugal and France. The reason for that is because people with a desire to inflict mass damage don't have quick access to the weapons needed to do it. If you're an American, it's as easy as buying a packet of cigarettes.

Question 40

In the second paragraph, the use of the term "deluded" is used to convey...

A – That pro-gun activists are crazy.

B – That people who believe the government will turn against them are misguided.

C – That people who believe their small firearms could protect them against the government are out of touch with reality.

D – That people who believe they can successfully rebel against the government are insane.

E – That pro-gun activists are all knowledgeable and cautious people.

Answer

Question 41

The author mentions the phrase "happy hunting, boys" to convey his message. What message is he trying to convey via this statement?

A – To warn that murderers and criminals would be extremely dangerous if given possession of guns.

B – To warn that murderers and criminals would damage the wildlife of the United States.

C – To warn that murderers and criminals would be subject to sadistic hunting games from law officers.

D – To warn that murderers and criminals might feel their rights have been violated.

E – To warn that female criminals would be discontented and would rise up against their male counterparts.

Answer

Question 42

The author compares buying a gun in the United States to "buying a packet of cigarettes". What is his purpose when doing this?

A – To demonstrate his dislike for cigarettes.

B – To demonstrate how easy it is to purchase a gun.

C – To hyperbolise the ease of buying a gun.

D – To demonstrate how easy it is to buy cigarettes.

E – To highlight the dangers of smoking.

Answer

ANSWERS TO MULTIPLE-CHOICE – SECTION 1

'The Prominence of Fernand Braudel'

Q1. A = 'To outline the influences of Braudel's works and discuss the differences of traditional theories'.

EXPLANATION = the author's main purpose is to explain the concepts behind Braudel's work, and discuss not only the influential factors that underline his thesis, but to challenge and discuss the differences between his work and the works of traditional theorists.

Q2. D = 'Point out the link between the increase in liberation and economics'.

EXPLANATION = the point of this question is for you to work out what the author has stated, and what has not. Within this passage, you should notice that the author does not mention the rise of liberation in reference to economics. The author does not refer to this link at all, and therefore it cannot be concluded from the passage.

Q3. E = 'Highlight initial assumptions made regarding Braudel's work on economics'.

EXPLANATION = the reason the author refers to other theorists Febrve and Bloch, is to highlight the inclinations they had regarding Braudel's work before it became influential. The passage clearly indicates that they "anticipated" Braudel's concepts prior to his works, and therefore the author uses this to highlight the importance of previous theories being expanded on and the assumptions made in relation to Braudel's theory.

Q4. C = 'History needs to be produced by focusing on the social sciences'.

EXPLANATION = the author uses the word "synthesise" in order to convey how history needs to be created and produced in relation to the social sciences. Answer option A can be ruled out because this offers a vague interpretation of the word. Answer option B can be ruled out because the term *social sciences* can be used in a variety of contexts and therefore does not offer the most plausible outcome. Answer option D can be ruled out because this is a too-strong assumption to make; the author does not mention that it is the *only* way. Answer option E can be ruled out because it does not offer any validity in relation to the word written in a meaningful context.

'The Distorted Views of the Media'

Q5. B = 'Publishers of newspapers are the people who decide what gets printed in their paper'.

EXPLANATION = the writer concludes from the passage that publishers focus on the importance of increasing their newspaper circulation, rather than maintaining efforts in regards to producing truthful and unbiased content. In order for the writer to come to this conclusion, the writer needs to assume that the publishers of the newspapers are the people in which decide what gets printed.

Q6. C = 'Irony'.

EXPLANATION = the author uses irony within the passage. The passage emphasises how the media continuously set out to convey an image that the majority of women are unable to obtain. Therefore this image continues to 'mock' society by conveying an image that they simply cannot live up to. The irony comes from the fact that the media are widely broadcasting images which do not reflect the large majority of the readership.

Q7. E = 'He doesn't think they reflect true beauty'.

EXPLANATION = the writer uses inverted commas around the words "ideal image" and "perfect woman" to emphasise his views on the subject matter. The use of these words does not represent fact; they represent opinions of the media that are continuously portrayed to society. Therefore, the use of the inverted commas are used to highlight the author's view that he doesn't take these words to be a true reflection of beauty, and instead, women are subjected to stereotyped views which is hoped by the media, to be the truth.

Q8. B = 'The media needs to be challenged in regards to stereotypical representations'.

EXPLANATION = the author compares women's body image with the representations of masculinity in order to illustrate how the media need to be challenged in regards to the stereotypical representations that are constantly conveyed as the truth. The author uses both these examples to demonstrate the influence of the media, and how the views in which are created by such mediums need to be confronted and challenged.

'Television Ads vs. Internet Ads'

Q9. D = 'The pace at which the two mediums evolve'.

EXPLANATION = the author clearly illustrates how the main difference between internet and television advertising is the pace at which the mediums evolve. The author goes on to discuss how television strategies have remained the same for years, using examples of time-scales and actors to emphasis their marketing approach. Whereas, the internet is described as an 'evolving and advanced' factor of technological changes, and therefore highlights how it is easier for the internet to meet the current needs and criteria of its audiences.

Q10. D = 'Highlight the growth and influences of online marketing'.

EXPLANATION = the term "burgeoning" can be defined as "beginning to grow or increase". Therefore, in the context of the phrase "capturing market share in *burgeoning* online economy", is used to highlight the growth and influence in which online marketing has to offer.

Q11. E = 'Is no longer the leading advertising platform'.

EXPLANATION = the author uses the evidence that the "internet accounts for over 23% of all advertising money", in order to demonstrate how television is no longer the leading advertising platform. Answer option A can be ruled out because the passage does not mention anything in regards to television no longer making money, therefore you cannot infer this to be true. Answer option B can be ruled out because the author does not suggest that television is no longer in demand, and therefore cannot be assumed. Answer option C can be ruled out because the author illustrates how television is no longer the leading marketing platform, therefore this is a contradictory statement of the overall passage. Answer option D can be ruled out because the author does not mention television as having 'died out', therefore this cannot be concluded.

'The Threats of Social Networking'

Q12. D = 'It provides suggestions to improve the issues as previously stated'.

EXPLANATION = the relationship between the last paragraph and the rest of the passage can best be described as "providing suggestions to improve the issues as previously stated". The author addresses several issues concerning social networking throughout the passage, and in the final paragraph, the author illustrates several suggestions of ways to improve or avoid the issues mentioned previously.

Q13. C = 'Guarded'.

EXPLANATION = the word that would best describe the tone of the author's writing in relation to his attitude concerning social networking is "guarded". The author offers very "guarded" responses in association with the importance of security for social networking sites. Answer options A and E are quite extreme, and the fact that the author is not overly *extreme* or *assertive* in his responses, suggests that these words cannot depict his overall tone of writing. Answer option D, 'upset', is not a word that best describes his attitudes; the author shows more of a concern then he does an upset, and therefore does not reflect his tone of voice. Answer option B, 'discouraged', does not reflect the overall tone of the author. This term is used to illustrate melancholy or somewhat disheartened, but the overall tone of the author does not come across as disheartened.

Q14. D = 'Schools, colleges and universities expressing concerns regarding their students and their behaviour'.

EXPLANATION = only answer option D is a statement that is not deemed a threat within the passage. All of the other answer options refer to parts of the passage which the author discusses.

Q15. E = 'Information founded online can be used as evidence in court'.

EXPLANATION = within the passage, the author *infers*, but does not state that "information founded online can be used as evidence in court". This must be correct due to the author using the evidence of photos being used in a court case that demonstrated underage drinking. Therefore the inference of using online information in court cases can be inferred.

'Global Warming'

Q16. B = 'We need to reduce our own carbon footprint'.

EXPLANATION = the writer infers that "we need to reduce our carbon footprint". We can ascertain this by establishing the point of the article, and ruling out other answers. For example, we know that the answer is not A, because it does not suggest global warming being on the increase. Neither is the answer D or E, because the writer gives limited mention to other living species, and would rather we acted to stop global warming rather than simply 'adapting and coping' with it. This leaves us with B and C. While it is fair to say that the writer does believe, to a large extent, that global warming is a man-made phenomenon; the purpose of the article is to resolve the issue instead of simply spreading blame. Therefore the answer is B, which points to a solution.

Q17. D = 'That the writer does not believe global warming to be of natural causes'.

EXPLANATION = the word "natural" is written inside inverted commas to suggest that "the writer does not believe global warming to be of natural causes". The writer clearly indicates a tone to his passage that places his argument against human activity and the impacts it has on the economy. Therefore the writer does not suggest global warming to be of a natural cause, and instead refers to climate change as a man-made phenomenon.

Q18. E = 'We do not show enough consideration and care towards our environment and social surroundings'.

EXPLANATION = from the passage, the writer infers but does not state, that "we do not show enough consideration and care towards our environment and social surroundings". Without this inference, the passage does not work. The writer demonstrates how man-made phenomenon is a direct cause of climate change and therefore suggests the lack of care we have regarding our planet.

'The 9/11 Terrorist Attack'

Q19. B = 'Power and Influence'.

EXPLANATION = according to the passage, the use of the word "symbolic", in relation to the twin towers, is used by the author to identify America as having power and influence. The passage clearly reiterates America as once being a powerful country contributing to the influences of both national and international interests. Whilst the other words could all be considered in relation to America, the passage clearly puts emphasis on the words "power and influence" to highlight how America was and still is perceived as powerful and influential.

Q20. E = 'The fourth plane, which was aimed at Washington but crashed in Pennsylvania, would have heavily increased the number of fatalities on the day'.

EXPLANATION= If we look at all of the other options, answer E is the most logical. There is no evidence in the passage that connects the attacks with a revolutionary act or political motivation, or anything that suggests that the government were at fault due to a lack of control or security measures. Therefore, the answer is E.

Q21. C = 'Attitudes regarding the significant consequences of an attack that ultimately affected the world forever'.

EXPLANATION = the last paragraph is written in conjunction with the passage to demonstrate the author's attitudes regarding the significant consequences of an attack that had global impact. The writer clearly emphasises the consequences of 9/11, and highlights his concerns in a particular way, by addressing the significant impacts of the attack, not just on America, but on a global scale.

'The Reign of Henry VIII'

Q22. B = 'Symbolism'.

EXPLANATION = the Hampton Court Palace is mentioned in conjunction with Henry VIII and Thomas Wolsey in order to highlight symbolic references of English culture.

Q23. A = 'Highlights a person who stands by religious attributes'.

EXPLANATION = the author uses the term "Defender of the Faith" to demonstrate someone who stands by religious attributes.

Q24. E = 'Aimed to reform the beliefs, traditions and practices of the Church'.

EXPLANATION = from the passage, we can assume that Protestant Reformation aimed to reform the beliefs, traditions and practices of the Church. From the passage, the author clearly illustrates the distinction between Henry VIII's views which often attacked others, including Martin Luther. The term reformation can be used to demonstrate the changes and renovations of something, in this instance it was in relation to religion, Protestants and the Church.

Q25. D = 'It goes against the male-domineering hierarchy of which women were not seen capable of ruling'.

EXPLANATION = in the fifth paragraph, the author discusses the importance of Henry VIII securing a son because "it goes against the male-domineering hierarchy of which women were not seen capable of ruling". The passage clearly indicates that prior to this time, there were no Queens that had ruled a country. The crowning of a woman was considered risky, and therefore Henry VIII was not going to let marital status claim the ruling title after his reign had ended, and to ensure this didn't happen, he needed to have a male heir.

'String Theory and Scientific Discoveries'

Q26. E = "…unifying".

EXPLANATION = the word used that does not highlight the negative qualities of string theory, is '…unifying'. All of the other words are used to demonstrate the ways in which string theory is flawed, and so the correct answer for this question is answer option E.

Q27. B = 'Reasoning assumes a causal connection without good evidence or support'.

EXPLANATION = the flaw in the concept of "The Theory of Everything" is that the reasoning assumes a causal connection without good evidence or support. In other words, string theory relies heavily on assumptions and experiments, but no proven hypotheses. Therefore, scientists are drawing to a supposition based on reasoning which may or may not be logical.

Q28. D = 'Suggest to the reader to understand string theory with considerable doubt and scepticism'.

EXPLANATION = the author uses the phrase "pinch of salt" to suggest to the reader that string theory needs to be considered with doubt and scepticism. The author illustrates how string theory is not proven, and therefore the reasoning and knowledge behind scientific discoveries in relation to string theory, should be carefully examined and doubted, due to the fact the research holds no clear scientific evidence.

Q29. C = 'Explain how the vibrations of a guitar are similar to that in string theory'.

EXPLANATION = the author compares string theory with a guitar in order to "explain how the vibrations of a guitar are similar to that in string theory". The passage clearly states that "a guitar is tuned by stretching and tweaking the strings that are under tension form vibrations", and depending on how that string is plucked, where you position your hands to cause tension, and how much tension is placed in the string initially, "will depend on the musical note that is played". The string needs to be put under tension in order to create some impact on the outcome, therefore identifying a similar effect.

'Propaganda, Power and Persuasion'

Q30. E = 'To illustrate a message aimed directly at the public'.

EXPLANATION = the use of the poster of Lord Kitchener pointing at its viewers is very persuasive. It is used to illustrate a message that is aimed directly at the public, in order to engage their attention, and allow them to be drawn in to the underlying messages of propaganda techniques.

Q31. E = 'To demonstrate how the public are inserted with information that is manipulated by those in power'.

EXPLANATION = the author compares propaganda as being similar to injections in order "to demonstrate how the public are inserted with information that is manipulated by those in power". In other words, the public are filled with messages and ideas based on what is conveyed to them. Unwittingly, the public are bombarded with these ideological views by which they then regard as the truth.

Q32. B = 'The moment people become aware of propaganda, it becomes ineffective'.

EXPLANATION = in the last paragraph, the author would most likely agree with the assumption that "the moment people become aware of propaganda, it becomes ineffective". The author highlights a clear point in the same passage that the public, more often than not, are oblivious to the fact that they are victims of propaganda. They are unable to see that the messages being sent to them, are the messages that have been carefully structured and manipulated in order of intent. But the author indicates how people who are fully aware of what is happening, are able to challenge these messages, and therefore make propaganda less effective.

'Creative Pedagogy'

Q33. C = 'Lateral thinker'.

EXPLANATION = the term "lateral thinker" best describes the author's perception of a critical learner. The passage clearly indicates that creativity and imagination are crucial for a child's development in regards to creative pedagogy. The use of the word "lateral" refers to imagination and innovation, and therefore best describes a person with a creative imagination.

Q34. B = 'The progression rate at which children develop'.

EXPLANATION = you could assume from the passage that Jean Piaget's work that individual learners differ from one another because of "the progression rate at which children develop". Piaget emphasises how children adapt to situations at various stages of their life and therefore suggests that children do not develop at the same pace.

Q35. A = 'Provide a more grounded knowledge of creative learning and imagination'.

EXPLANATION = the author uses the word "holistic" to provide a more grounded knowledge of creative learning and imagination. The passage constantly refers to the importance of creative thinking and imagination, and therefore the use of the word "holistic", means that a complete knowledge of learning can be achieved through innovative thoughts and creative ideas.

Q36. C = 'Explain the mechanisms and structures by which children develop using reasoning and hypotheses'.

EXPLANATION = according to the passage, Piaget's overall aim in regards to his works on children development, is to "explain the mechanisms and structures by which children develop using reasoning and hypotheses". Piaget demonstrates his observations on children has proven a useful way to interact with children on their level, and understand what the processes are of which a child goes through in terms of learning developments.

'Children Becoming Teenagers'

Q37. D = 'The transformation and changes from a child into a teenager'.

EXPLANATION = the use of the word "metamorphosed" is used to highlight "the transformation and changes from a child into a teenager". The passage specifically discusses the changes children face when dealing with the struggles of adolescence, and therefore illustrates how these changes modify the way we see a child, who is on the verge of 'growing up'.

Q38. A = 'You cannot hide the difficulties of raising a teenager'.

EXPLANATION = the author uses the phrase, "I am not going to sugar coat it" in order to convey that "you cannot hide the difficulties of raising a teenager". The author states the complexities of raising a teenager and therefore illustrates how the author is not hiding away from the truths, despite how unappealing they may be.

Q39. E = 'Past memories belonging to the parent'.

EXPLANATION = the author uses the phrase, "only shadows remain…" in order to convey the thoughts of "past memories belonging to the parent". The author discusses their child as a 'baby' and therefore reflects back on past memories. The fact that their child is changing into a young adult, demonstrates how the thoughts of them being a 'baby', is no longer appropriate and therefore act solely as distant memories of childhood.

'Concealed Weaponry and the Public'

Q40. C = 'That people who believe their small firearms could protect them against the government are out of touch with reality'.

EXPLANATION = the term "deluded" is used to show that people who believe their small firearms could protect them against the government are out of touch with reality. We know that this is the answer because the passage makes specific reference to the word 'physical resistance' which implies a need for protection. Therefore, the answer is C.

Q41. A = 'To warn that murderers and criminals would be extremely dangerous if given possession of guns'.

EXPLANATION = the author uses sarcasm to warn that murderers and criminals would be extremely dangerous if given possession of guns, and would likely begin to hunt and kill innocent civilians.

Q42. C = 'To hyperbolise the ease of buying a gun'.

EXPLANATION = the author hyperbolises the ease of buying a gun, by comparing it to buying a packet of cigarettes. Buying a gun is not quite as simple as buying cigarettes, but by exaggerating how easy it is to get hold of one; the author shows strong emphasis to his point.

MULTIPLE-CHOICE
(SECTION 2)

Disclaimer: *The content within this guide does not reflect the views of any person associated with, or working for, How2Become. They are solely intended to instigate debate and discussion, to help you practice for the Law National Admissions Test.*

You have 95 minutes in which to read the 12 passages and answer all 42 questions.

1. The Future of Education

Educational institutions have changed considerably over the last few years. Recently, textbooks have been pushed aside in favour of technological advances; such as computers, laptops and tablets. The effect of this is that children are now more prone to seeking information from technology sources, rather than textbooks themselves.

With more institutions using tablets and laptops, it is apparent that textbooks will continue to decline, and will ultimately be pushed out altogether. The common public understanding is that tablets contain more information than books and so they are a better source of information; a thought that I believe to be ridiculous.

The notion of implementing new technologies into academia is absurd. The fact that children are growing up in a world engrossed with the concepts of new technology, has led to a collective 'dumbing down' of society. Our society has become so engrossed with the internet that it is failing to prevent its youngest members from recognising the biggest misconceptions of online information. They are being given information which sometimes misconstrues the facts and truth.

Whilst you need to look at both sides of the coin, I believe that it is inevitable that technology will continue to advance, and will subsequently replace all other modes of communication that are considered 'out-of-date' and 'old-fashioned'. Yes, technology has its uses, and yes it provides a fast and efficient way of maintaining information, but the fact is, students are unaware of the issues this can impose on their academic studies.

As tablets have become more prevalent, a new debate has formed which argues that tablets should replace all of the textbooks used in schools. Whilst teachers argue that using tablets offer a lighter and more accessible means of reading information, it is questionable as to whether today's students are capable of using the tablets to research effectively and determine which sources are reliable.

Many people believe that children are becoming too obsessed with the latest technologies. Working-class families in particular struggle with this, as they do not have the means to supply their children with these electronic luxuries. Not only are tablets costly and easy to break, but they can have a profound impact on children's health. Tablets can cause headaches, eyestrain, blurred vision and other long term health problems.

The future of education hangs in the balance, and may well be decided by the battle between standard books, and the implementation of new technology. I believe that technology is overrated, and belittles the information sources that we have used for hundreds of years. Why change now? There is nothing wrong with our books.

Question 1

The author uses the phrase "to look at both sides of the coin", in order to…

A – Demonstrate how it is difficult to distinguish between both sides of the argument.

B – Address both sides of the argument, before forming a conclusion.

C – Analyse the counter-arguments in order to reject their conclusions.

D – Suggest how it is important to gain as much information as possible before reaching a conclusion.

E – Gain a better overall view of a situation.

Answer

Question 2

The author *implies*, but does not state, how…

A – Children are more interactive when using technology.

B – Children do not engage with learning if given a textbook to read.

C – Children are better off with educational technology, as opposed to textbooks.

D – Children are becoming too reliant on technology.

E – Children are too naïve to see the consequences of using technology.

Answer

Question 3

The author uses the idea of a "dumbing down" of society, to highlight how…

A – Technology is the cause of a less-educated society.
B – Information founded online is incorrect.
C – Textbooks are the only truthful source which can be relied upon.
D – Technology plays a vital role in producing incorrect or misleading information.
E – Children are spending too much time engaging with technology.

Answer

Question 4

The author's tone of voice throughout the passage regarding technology usage in education, is…

A – Antagonistic.
B – Hostile.
C – Neutral.
D – Indifferent.
E – Incredulous.

Answer

2. Obesity and Culture

It is fair to say that the media are obsessed with the idea of an "ideal image". A beautiful young woman with curves in all of the right places, great hair, perfect complexion and sparkling confidence; or a man with bulging biceps, a rippling stomach and the perfect combination of masculinity, pride and appearance.

Yet when we look out the window, much to our disappointment, we are shown a society of citizens in all shapes and sizes, that rarely live up to these expectations. More concerns have arisen over the rise in obesity, and how obesity has become a significant part of contemporary culture.

It is often debated as to whether or not obesity should be considered as a disability. Should people who suffer with obesity get the same level of rights in terms of discrimination laws? These laws act as a shield for people with learning difficulties, wheelchair users, hearing disabilities, the visually impaired etc. To what extent can obesity be classed as a disability? Is it a disability, or is it simply a result of poor lifestyle choices?

I struggle to understand people who have issues concerning their weight, but do little to help, prevent or find out the cause. Many individuals that suffer from obesity have other health issues, which in turn affect their weight. Issues from childhood, unpleasant experiences or mental instabilities can have a profound effect on a person's weight gain; it is important to understand the reasons behind weight gain, in order to deal with the overall issue.

Although obesity can be related to other health issues, many people refuse to accept that they need help and thus do little to help themselves in the long-term. Calling obesity a disability does not fix this problem. In the majority of cases, a person is able to rectify their behaviour and eating habits by dealing with other issues that have led to their increased weight.

Lifestyle is a huge factor which needs to be considered in relation to obesity. In many cases, obesity is brought on by the individual themselves. It is preventable, and therefore should not be classed as a disability. To define obesity as a disability, would create controversial problems with people who *actually* have a disability that isn't a direct result of their lifestyle choices.

Suggesting obesity to be a form of disability is a preposterous notion. It is unfair to people who have had to live with a disability that is out of their hands. Obesity is the result of sedentary lifestyles, and the actions of individuals who continue to eat the wrong foods and perform little exercise; "couch potatoes" in other words. How can these people be classified as having a disability? The fact that obesity can be prevented and reduced, suggests that the idea of labelling it as a disability, is ludicrous.

Question 5

From reading the first and second paragraph, the author uses a literary technique to compare the "ideal image" with real life experience. Which of the following *best* describes the literary technique?

A – Oxymoron.

B – Analogy.

C – Bathos.

D – Imagery.

E – Irony.

Answer [   ]

Question 6

What is the *underlying assumption* in the fourth paragraph?

A – Lifestyle choices are the underlying factor of obesity.

B – Obesity is a lifestyle choice.

C – Psychological problems are the underlying factor of obesity.

D – Obesity can be prevented.

E – It is important to understand the emotional states caused by obesity.

Answer [   ]

Question 7

The author has written the word *"actually"*, in italics because...

A – Obesity cannot be proven to be a disability.
B – The author agrees with obesity being a disability.
C – The author highlights how obesity should not be considered a disability.
D – The author is demonstrating the importance of the paragraph.
E – Obesity is not a justified lifestyle choice.

Answer

Question 8

In the last paragraph, the author refers to the term "couch potato". What is the literary technique used here?

A – Allusion.
B – Colloquialism.
C – Amplification.
D – Hyperbole.
E – Juxtaposition.

Answer

3. Natural Laws

There is a marked difference between the laws of nature, and the laws made by man. I really frown upon the term "natural law". The underlying idea that law and morality are separate elements is somewhat bogus, and I find it improbable to talk about one without referring to the other.

I often take it upon myself to engage with law as a means of moral demonstration. How then, can we begin to decipher between law and morality? The truth remains that behind every law is a value, a belief, a thought process that accounts for our perception of what we view to be right, and what we view to be wrong. The laws of nature come with great ideas, illusions and beliefs that we often use to create meaning and interpretation. The two elements are interlinked and are needed to draw upon assumptions that rely on a combination of thoughts and ideas, with environments, nature and surroundings.

Laws of nature do not act as commands, but instead act as a declaration which we choose to follow. The use of the word 'law' in this context doesn't seem right. Natural law, often referred to as the laws of nature, can be defined as a system of rules and decrees that are determined by the natures of the universe. It is in my opinion, that these "laws" should not be classed as such, and instead should be regarded as uniformities and standards which we choose whether to accept or not.

Natural laws are a way of establishing moral boundaries. Yet, it also acts as a legal theory that proves difficult to intersect. There are different perceptions that have been theorised in relation to natural laws, and many theorists choose to "sit on the fence" in regards to arguing against other thesis.

Certainly, when we look at morals in association with laws, values and ideologies, it is difficult to determine what is 'right'. The elementary fallacies that circulate within the nature of laws convey different morals for different cultures. This is particularly accurate in pluralistic societies such as ours, whereby it is only acceptable to have one wife, whereas in Muslim cultures, it is acceptable to have multiple. The conflict between morality and law proves problematic, and therefore defining these rules as 'laws' is illogical.

The nature of law is often invoked in criticism that widely disputes judicial decisions about what the law says is lawful. There are several theories of natural law, each differing with respects of the role in which morality plays, and ultimately determines the authority and sanctions of legal norms.

I struggle to comprehend natural law. The arguments of such laws remain coherent, yet I fail to understand the common misconceptions within a pluralistic society. They rest heavily on metaphysical presuppositions which I find difficult to decipher. With every word, there is meaning. With every action, there is a motive. With every law, there are boundaries. I find myself struggling to grasp these two elements as nothing more than elements in conjunction, which rely heavily on one another to create some form of logic and understanding.

Question 9

The term "natural law" is implied as...

A – Rigid.
B – Ambiguous.
C – Unreasonable.
D – Defective.
E – Unalterable.

Answer [   ]

Question 10

The author conveys the term "law" in regards to natural laws, as being...

A – Adaptable.
B – Substantiated.
C – Inflexible and punitive.
D – Assuming and pretentious.
E – Constructive.

Answer [   ]

Question 11

According to the passage, the author refers to natural law in what type of approach?

A – Sociological.
B – Psychological.
C – Educational.
D – Philosophical.
E – Pragmatic.

Answer [   ]

4. Covering Disasters

European media coverage of natural disasters from around the globe is often disputed in regards to its validity. It is remarkable that nations choose to frame certain events based on whether citizens from that nation were effected by the disaster; rather than simply looking at the event from an unbiased viewpoint.

Natural disasters not only affect the local community, but also play a significant role in terms of global news. Natural disasters often involve immediate deaths which toll from just a few loss of lives, to hundreds of thousands. The Boxing Day Tsunami of 2004 is just one example of how a natural disaster can dominate media coverage, particularly across newspapers. An event on such a large scale is often subject to news stories that focus on citizens of the country in which news is reported. If a train derailed in France, English reporters are more likely to centre their story on any English citizens that were affected, in order to appeal to its targeted national audience.

Journalism is at the forefront of every major disaster, and without it we would live in a world of obliviousness and serenity, without any actual knowledge of the goings-on around us. The media is used to build up an image of the short and long term repercussions of such disasters, as well as the aftermath and culture of those affected.

While we choose to believe everything that we read in newspapers because it is written as "evidence", the fact remains that we are simply voyeurs through the looking glass that is provided to us at the moment an event takes place. Despite their lack of reflexivity, newspapers maintain a way of interpreting the event in a way that everyone would understand, if they had witnessed it for themselves.

We continue to accept journalism because it's all we know. Despite its lack of objectivity, morality, interpretation and truth, it has and probably always will be, the centre of our information source. Without which, events like tsunamis, earthquakes, volcanic eruptions and floods, would no longer be recognised as global events.

Not only are newspapers and other forms of media coverage used to "break news", but they are often used as a form of communication that allows people to understand the ramifications of events on society, culture and contemporary journalism. We are moved by what we are shown, and at first instance we are made to believe one interpretation that is given to us, in order to convey something in a particular way. I have spent many years too, believing that everything we are shown is shown to us for a reason. However, maturity and experience has led me to believe that something is shown to us merely to cause a reaction, to stir up events, to provide a holistic view of the way in which we should perceive the world.

Question 12

Within the first passage, what assumption can be made from the author's interpretation of media coverage of international events?

A – More natural events occur in foreign countries.

B – European Governments are actively involved in the press of natural events.

C – Europe judges international events based on the number of Europeans affected.

D – Natural disasters have a global impact.

E – Foreign countries need Europe's help in the aftermath of such disasters.

Answer

Question 13

In the fourth paragraph, the author uses the word "reflexivity" to demonstrate…

A – The impact that natural disasters have on the rest of society.

B – A truth and overview of the current events that take place, which we are unable to witness for ourselves.

C – A hidden agenda that is present in news stories in order to make them more believable.

D – The relationship between cause and effect.

E – The type of reaction that journalists are trying to produce, when they portray a natural disaster in a particularly deceptive or engaging way.

Answer

Question 14

In paragraph four, the author chooses to put the term 'evidence', in inverted commas. Which of the following *best* addresses why the author has done this?

A – To distinguish the importance of hard "evidence" in relation to news stories.

B – To highlight the authors interpretation of evidence lacking credibility and sincerity.

C – To reinforce how journalism does not always report the truth.

D – To highlight how the author is incredulous of the role of journalism of international events.

E – To suggest the implications of news stories reported locally, and news storied reported internationally.

Answer

Question 15

The author uses the expression "voyeurs through the looking glass" to *best* describe how…

A – The media are the instigators of social events becoming world wide phenomena.

B – The media act as a 'looking glass' to help society engage with social events from around the world.

C – International events rely on media coverage in order to be established in other countries.

D – Western culture is centred on maintaining news stories that reflect international events.

– The victims of international disasters use the media as a way of gaining access to the rest of society.

Answer

5. Same-Sex Marriage and Society

It is about time that society got off their high horse, and understood the ramifications of preventing the rights to legalised same-sex marriages. With a gay brother and homosexual friends within my social circle, I find it preposterous that society has evolved and adapted to cater for advances in technology, teenage pregnancy, riots and civil disputes, and yet we continue to live in a world that continues to mock and frown upon those dissimilar to us.

There is no doubt that attitudes regarding same-sex marriage have softened since it first came about. The legislation for gay marriage was passed in 2014 for England, Scotland and Wales, but continues to be contested in Northern parts of Ireland.

Within the first three months of same-sex marriage becoming legalised in the UK, over 1,400 ceremonies were conducted for gay marriages. This has led to powerful signals that promote gay marriage as loving and committed, and shows British culture as respecting and tolerant.

As a child, we are continuously told to pursue our dreams, and to be "ourselves". If a person then grows up choosing to follow the path of being gay, they should have the right to do so. They should not be prone to disgruntled glances and constant remarks behind their backs. Gay people should not feel as though they are 10 years old and back on the playground, defending themselves. They should be able to feel mature and accepted for the person they have chosen to be, and indulge in a lifestyle that doesn't affect anyone but themselves.

Its consistency with scripture in regards to religion, culture and tradition is believed to be downplayed in order to make the 'act' immoral and unacceptable. Yet, what people fail to notice is that love is defined by God as "where love is, there is God also". Therefore, this belittles the argument what people choose to believe in, in regards to religion and its values.

Not only do same-sex marriages offer variety, but individuals are more inclined to prove that they deserve the same rights as everybody else. They are correlated with lower divorce rates, provide stability in association to marital status, and bring financial gain to its government and boost economy, so why then do they continue to be ridiculed?

The fact that our society is constantly changing, means that the concept of marital traditions need to change also. Traditions claim how marriage can only be defined through a man and a woman. People are held back by the past and struggle to comprehend the adaptations in Western society.

A person should be with the person they wish to spend their life with, the same way a person chooses to have a baby, or have cosmetic surgery, or chooses to donate blood... all of these maintain shed loads of values or ideologies that people regard to be wrong or right, and therefore it should be no different. A person's choice, is a person's life. It is up to them to choose how they define themselves.

Question 16

Which of the following words, *best* addresses the qualities the author is trying to display when comparing thoughts of 'gay people' and 'playgrounds'?

A – Cheerful, ignorant, oblivious.

B – Inexperienced, different, affectionate.

C – Childish, immature, ignorant.

D – Confident, tolerant, curious.

E – Sociable, oblivious, different.

Answer

Question 17

The term "scripture" in context of the fifth passage, suggests...

A – The formal writings which are regarded as truth.

B – The rules and regulations given by religion.

C – Understandings of the expectations required in society.

D – The sacred writings of religious views.

E – Verbal understandings that are passed down to generation to generation.

Answer

Question 18

What is the *main* assumption that can be made from the second paragraph?

A – Everybody is against same-sex marriage.
B – Many people continue to have doubts about same-sex marriages.
C – Some people continue to have doubts about gay marriage.
D – Few people have doubts about gay marriage.
E – Nobody has doubts against same-sex marriage.

Answer

6. Doping in Sports

In recent years, a topic of popular debate is to what extent do drugs need restricting? These questions are not just limited to those who have a drug addiction, or those who take drugs for recreational usage, but also for sports players and athletes.

The use of artificial enhancements and banned substances in sport is commonly known as 'doping'. These substances enhance an athlete's performance, in order to help them gain an advantage over their competition. The act of doping fundamentally diminishes the spirit of the sport and what it represents. Sports act as both professional and recreational fun. Athletes who belittle the name of sport make it difficult to maintain a representation of sport as truthful, clean and fair.

The concept of doping has become an increased concern in recent years, with many athletes choosing to use banned substances as a way of extending their careers. Not only does this affect the overall perception of the sport, but they fail to see the underlying consequences that this has in terms of their health. Doping through the use of stimulants makes an athlete more alert and masks their fatigue. However it also has the dangerous side effect of causing long-term heart failure. Stimulants are addictive, and therefore a person can become heavily reliant on continuous usage, causing greater health risks.

The use of drugs to enhance a person's sporting performance dates back hundreds of years, and has been a concern in a variety of sporting activities. The ancient Olympics held in Greece was rumoured to have been riddled of doping activity. With little success, sporting organisations and federations have attempted to prevent athletes from using drugs. Unfortunately, there are now more news stories than ever before concerning athletes who have been banned from their sport because of drug use.

Doping does not just affect professional athletes. More and more people who participate in some form of amateur sporting activity are taking performance enhancing drugs. Younger people are prone to look up to these stars, and therefore can become influenced by the actions of these athletes and thus imitate their behaviour and choices in regards to drug use.

There needs to be a concerted and regulated approach to doping, in order to decrease the use of prohibited substances and strengthen the general perception of sport through respect, admiration and honour. However, I struggle to see how these drugs can be stopped altogether. I think it is necessary to address this issue with the utmost determination and regulation to prevent doping as much as possible.

Question 19

What is the author's *main* argument of the overall passage?

A – Doping threatens the perception of the sport.
B – Doping threatens the athletes career.
C – Doping creates issues regarding health and safety.
D – Doping creates an awareness of banned substances.
E – Doping threatens the overall integrity of the sport.

Answer

Question 20

According to the *main* passage, what is the main inference which demonstrates the importance of the nature of a sport?

A – Economic growth.
B – Role models.
C – Appreciation.
D – Reputation.
E – Veracity.

Answer

Question 21

What word *best* describes the term 'doping', in context of sporting events?

A – Unethical.
B – Indispensable.
C – Problematic.
D – Nonsensical.
E – Perilous.

Answer [   ]

7. Medical Marijuana

I am no stranger to occasional aches and pains, and I know the impact this can have on day-to-day activities. It is with that in mind, that I feel obligated to state that I believe all people with 'real' illnesses should be allowed to take marijuana as a form of medication, or at least, given the option.

Every day for over a year, I observed the affect that chemotherapy has on a life. I watched as cancer took over a body so young and full of life. Nose bleeds, vomiting and constant changes in body temperature were just some of the many side effects of the disease.

Medical marijuana is a form of medical cannabis that alleviates symptoms and reduces severe pain. The use of marijuana as a medical intervention is somewhat uncontroversial when used in dealing with cancer patients, people with a long-term illness or a child who suffers with convulsions. Nobody disputes the use of cannabis in these instances, because it is seen as the right thing to do.

It is between medical practitioners and their patients to choose whether they need marijuana in order to cope with the symptoms or illnesses with which they live. Who are we to prevent people from feeling better? Who are we to tell someone what they should or should not do to ease their pain? No one, that's who. We do not have the right to prolong the terrible and painful experiences of people who suffer on a daily basis, and it is up to us to persuade institutions that despite the lack of evidence, it is a choice that needs to be taken seriously.

Of course, details need to be addressed to determine the severity of a person's case and whether they are eligible to take 'medical marijuana'. It has already been proven to decrease the side effects of chemotherapy. Chemotherapy often causes severe vomiting and nausea in cancer patients, and the use of marijuana provides effective relief from such symptoms.

Improving the quality of life doesn't come easy, and if a situation allows a person to gain improvements, then it is my opinion that they should be open to all possibilities, including intakes of marijuana as a medical intervention. If it gives a person the chance to ameliorate fatigue, restore appetites, reduce pain and discomfort, and ultimately live a better life, I whole-heartedly concur with the use of marijuana in such circumstances.

Like I said before, I am no stranger to such events, and it would be hypocritical of me to believe in the benefits of using marijuana if I had no experience. But in actual fact I do. I mentioned before about overlooking all the signs whilst a person dealt with the implications of chemo, when in actual fact, that person was me. I find it remarkable how little people know about the extremities in which people face with and have to deal with every day, and to be given the opportunity to make each day that little bit easier by reducing the side effects, fills my thoughts with hope and belief.

Question 22

What tone *best* describes the voice in which the author uses when discussing whether medical marijuana should be made legal?

A – Apprehensive.

B – Emphatic.

C – Confident.

D – Sympathetic.

E – Intense.

Answer

Question 23

The author uses a first person approach, in order to...

A – Understand the sensitive issues of drugs and health.

B – Gain an emotional response from readers.

C – Put the readers in a position of someone else's shoes.

D – Determine the impact of chemotherapy.

E – Convey how important it is for the reader to address health issues.

Answer

Question 24

From reading the passage, it is *inferred*, but not stated that...

A – Marijuana is illegal in all countries.

B – Marijuana is a tried and tested method that fails to show health benefits.

C – Marijuana is accepted as a form of medication in some places.

D – Marijuana is a tried and tested method that has proved of assistance to long-term illnesses.

E – Marijuana is politically unacceptable which Governments find morally wrong.

Answer

Question 25

The *main* flaw of this argument, is that it relies heavily on...

A – Cause and effect.

B – Too many assumptions.

C – Personal involvement.

D – Restricting the options of other possibilities.

E – Confuses necessary and sufficient conditions.

Answer

8. Universities and Higher Paying Job Offers

A Graduates from a university of a higher ranking, are more likely to be granted jobs of a higher position. Students from universities such as Oxford or Cambridge, are shown to be more likely to gain senior roles within well-established British institutions. Not only that, but graduates from these top-leading universities tend to earn a higher salary than a person who graduated from a less prestigious university. It may not be fair, but attending a top ranked university will provide greater chances of gaining better job positions with higher earning potential.

B A degree is a degree, is it not? Why then, should it matter where a student chooses to study for their further education? The point is that everyone goes to university for the same reason, to gain a higher education in order to secure a better job title. The years spent at university prove convenient in equipping students with the essential life skills and qualities required for the real world by creating mature, educated and well-rounded citizens. If students work hard, they should reap the benefits. It is up to society to maintain a well-rounded group of citizens who are hard-working, motivated and willing to learn.

C Education no longer guarantees anyone a solid future. Students continue to go to university simply because they would find it a struggle to become employed. The lack of available jobs has had a huge impact on the younger generation, and they gain no security or job future even after attending university. Some jobs do not employ people with university degrees, because they are deemed 'overqualified'. Going to university in this day and age is a waste of time for both students and the government. Not only that, but it also wastes money which is given to students for tuition fees and student loans, and ultimately affects the growth rate of the economy, with more students "hanging about" and waiting to make their next move, even though the future does not guarantee them employment.

D Work experience gained during university years, can be hugely advantageous to graduates looking for employment. Employers are no longer basing their choices on education qualifications or the best scores. Incentives from higher authorities have become increasingly focused on internships and work experience placements for graduates who wish to obtain a better job after their university years. It is no wonder that people are choosing not to go to university, and instead choosing to join the world of work as soon as possible. Gaining experience demonstrates not only your willingness to engage with the job role prior to an actual job position, but also your commitment, eagerness and positive attitude to work, unpaid if necessary, in order to gain a foot in the door and put yourself ahead of others.

Question 26

From author A's argument, what can you *assume* from their passage?

A – Social status makes for better education.

B – Attending a prestigious university allows graduates to earn more because of the university status.

C – You will be unable to gain the same status and respect if you attend a university other than Oxford or Cambridge.

D – Choosing your university is extremely important regarding social status.

E – Jobs choose graduates based on merit and experience.

Answer

Question 27

What is the hypothetical reasoning used in author B's passage?

A – 'A degree is a degree, is it not?'

B – 'The point is everyone goes to university for the same reasons – to gain a higher education and gain a better job'.

C – 'Why then, should it matter where a student decides to study for their further education?'

D – 'It is up to society, to maintain a well-rounded group of citizens that are hardworking, motivated and show continuous willing to learn'.

E – 'If students work hard, they should receive the benefits'.

Answer

Question 28

The use of the term "hanging out" in context of author C's passage, is used to suggest...

A – Students are lingering in education because of uncertainties regarding future careers.

B – Students have nothing better to do.

C – Students are bored with education.

D – Students are prolonging the experiences of working in the real world.

E – Students choose to go to university because they *want* to, not because they *have* to.

Answer

9. Legal Highs

Like any mother, I find it impossible to keep watch of my children 24/7. I have two boys, aged 14 and 21, and the more I think about what they're getting up to, the more it frightens me.

I have come to terms with the impact of legal highs and how they have life-threatening implications. What teenagers fail to realise is how these substances, despite being legal, can have the same affect as if you were to take cannabis, cocaine or other illegal drugs. I feel as though I have the right to speak out, based on the experience that resulted in my eldest son being hospitalised.

Health institutions should not spend their time and efforts on people who break the law and take drugs. Although legal highs are not breaking the law, these drugs are not meant for human consumption.

Failing to understand the implications of such drug use can have profound consequences. These psychoactive substances or 'club drugs' are not covered by any law in regards to misuse or illegal usage. I find it extremely frightening that no preventative measures have been enforced.

Despite these drugs being marketed as legal, it does not mean that they are by any means safe, acceptable or approved. Due to a lack of direct testing, there is no scientific evidence to suggest the harm or effect that these drugs could have on the human body. These drugs should not be named 'legal highs'. This is wrong and misleading, and is proving to be extremely harmful, particularly for the younger generation. Side effects such as drowsiness, paranoia, comas, seizures and even death are enough reason to ban these substances and make them illegal.

Extensive investigation of these substances has revealed that they are becoming stronger, and more addictive. Worryingly, they are becoming more addictive than most illegal drugs, which demonstrates a clear need for maintenance and regulation. Legal highs are not for human consumption and are not marketed in that way. Instead, they are legalised substances which form incenses, salts or plant food that subsequently belittle the law, and make them acceptable.

The label of legal highs needs to be changed in order to prevent serious health risks for humans. These substances need to be banned because they cause as much harm to people as any illegal drug.

Question 29

What is the *main* conclusion which the author makes?

A – The risks of legal highs need to be taken more seriously by the younger generation.

B – The uncertain health implications of legal highs, combined with their accessibility, presents a major challenge and risk to the public's health.

C – Legal drugs contain the same ingredients as illegal substances, but are disguised through different marketing outlets, such as plant food.

D – Parents need to take more control in their children's lives, and reduce any risk of legal high consumption.

E – Legal highs affect the social order of society, and have dire consequences on financial, social, cultural, and ideological views of contemporary society.

Answer

Question 30

The tone of voice that the author uses when discussing the implications of the term 'legal highs', is...

A – Disappointed.

B – Indifferent.

C – Dismayed.

D – Concerned.

E – Alarmed.

Answer

Question 31

The use of the term "psychoactive" substances, is used to illustrate...

A – The profanities that can cause a person to seek activity and adrenaline.

B – How these substances can cause health risks such as palpitations and stress.

C – The change in body functions that ultimately affect the heart and circulatory system.

D – How these substances can cause changes in brain function, which result in altered perception, attitude and behaviour.

E – The change in body including increased hormone levels and alterations in brain function.

Answer

Question 32

From the third paragraph, the conclusion that people using legal highs or illegal drugs should not receive treatment, can *best* be supported by what reasoning?

A – The Government does not have the means to fund a person's drug addiction.

B – People take drugs as a way of escapism and therefore cannot help their addiction.

C – Giving people treatment is unfair on others who deserve it.

D – Treatments are expensive and should be given to those who do not break the law.

E – People should not be treated for self-inflicted issues.

Answer

10. Combat Sport

Combat sports, also known as fighting sports, have been in existence for thousands of years. There are many different forms of these sports, but all involve a pre-arranged set of rules and fighting techniques, which are used to determine a winner.

With such sporting events, comes serious risks. The aggressive nature of combat sports can raise extreme ethical issues. We are taught as a child that violence is bad, and that we shouldn't use aggressive behaviour as a means of resolution. Yet from an early age, school children have access to a variety of competitive, and dangerous fighting sports.

Sports including boxing, kickboxing, wrestling, judo, martial arts and jujitsu, are all types of combat sport. Combatants are trained in using techniques to subdue their opponent. Thus, we must ask ourselves an important question: how ethical are such sports? Even young girls are being taught to defend themselves from an early age, which highlights how combat is deemed 'the norm'.

It can be argued that less aggressive sports that contain reckless behaviour such as football and rugby sometimes result in injury. Yet, these teams and people do not win the game by implementing any force or aggression; they win because of the number of goals or points they score. Whereas, combat sports intentionally set out to fight and defeat an opponent. In these sports, you can only win by causing enough conflict for a combatant to be unable to continue.

Some people believe that the vast amount of training and techniques that go into particular fighting sports, make them less harmful on society than many people think. Licensing sports where children, teenagers and even adults can put their aggression into a sport that is filled with many rules and boundaries, is far healthier than having no outlet to unleash their anger. Contrary to this belief, it can also be argued that children who are constantly exposed to violent and aggressive behaviour will display negative long-term developmental effects, skewed social behaviour and ideas about what is right and wrong. If a child is taught to fight in order to protect themselves from losing, how can they recognise when it is safe to do this? At school? On the playground? Playing with their siblings? No, you wouldn't expect a child to use aggressive behaviour in any of these situations, but a child's learning process is somewhat different to ours. Therefore they will be unable to distinguish between situations that require certain types of behaviour i.e. acceptable behaviour in different types of sports, and everyday behaviour at home, in the classroom, on the playground etc.

Question 33

In paragraph three, what is the *underlying assumption* of the sentence 'even young girls are being taught to defend themselves from an early age'?

A – Young girls are considered weak.

B – Young girls are considered vulnerable.

C – Young girls need to experience the same developments as boys.

D – They need to learn combat to build strength and confidence.

E – There is something to defend from.

Answer

Question 34

What is the significant difference between combat sports and 'less aggressive sports'?

A – The aims of the sport.

B – The people who play the sport.

C – The perception of the sport.

D – The integrity of the sport.

E – The impacts shown in the sport.

Answer

Question 35

In the final paragraph, the author states, "If a child is taught to fight in order to protect themselves from losing, how can they recognise when it is safe to do this? At school? On the playground? Playing with their siblings?" What is the name for the literary device used in the above sentences?

A – Onomatopoeia.
B – Symbolism.
C – Irony.
D – Rhetorical Questioning.
E – Pathos.

Answer

Question 36

Comparing combat sport, with less aggressive sports such as football and rugby, is used to emphasis…

A – Symbolism.
B – A metaphor.
C – An analogy.
D – An anecdote.
E – An oxymoron.

Answer

11. Tourism in the Developing World

A Traditionally, tourism was used as a form of escapism, where people could forget their problems by exploring the world. Now, tourism has become a rapidly growing industry and plays a huge role in economic growth.

B The mounting fears that are often associated with tourism in today's society surround the way in which it impacts the developing world. The developing world is defined by the amount of gross national income that decides which stage of development a country is at. Countries that are less economically and technically advanced, are considered as 'Third World'. South-East/Central Asia and Eastern/Western Africa are commonly regarded as some of the most deprived and underprivileged regions in the world.

C Some people believe that mass tourism is exploitive to Third World countries. With more and more people choosing to venture across the world, developing countries are popular tourist destinations. While these countries are steadily becoming more recognised by the global populous, they continue to struggle in terms of social, cultural and financial understandings.

D In order to aid Third World countries, tourism needs to engage with the promotion of growth and development in not only the rural areas of countries, but also with women, youth and the environment. Mass tourism has been blamed for exploiting poorer countries, and endangering biodiversity. Tourism is frequently blamed for using up these countries limited resources, in an inefficient and wasteful manner.

E The bottom line is that tourism allows for countries who are not as fortunate as us to create better equality and help eradicate exploitation. Countries such as Rwanda are just one of many countries that have been subject to the benefits of tourism. Not only has it reduced poverty and hunger, it allows children to go to school, and helps them grow their economy. It allows for higher powers to generate and encourage tourism by addressing important issues such as poverty and deprivation.

F Tourism is a great way to raise awareness of particular global plights, and to allow more developed nations to help sustain peace and stability in Third World countries. Tourism allows for the creation of jobs, generate income, improve local lifestyles, and ultimately create a better diversity.

Question 37

Which author highlights the importance of possible Government intervention?

A – Author A.
B – Author B.
C – Author C.
D - Author D.
E – Author E.

Answer

Question 38

In author D's paragraph, what is the *main* conclusion?

A – The tourism industry has transformed societies for the better.
B – The tourism industry has had no profound effect on third world countries.
C – The tourism industry helps Third World countries to develop into First World countries.
D – The tourism industry has helped transform societies for the worst.
E – The tourism industry has had a huge impact on Third World countries.

Answer

Question 39

The collective implication of the main benefit of tourism, is that tourism...

A – Improves the financial state of the economy.
B – Improves the social infrastructures of society.
C – Allows host communities to become more recognised.
D – Helps poorer countries to form allegiances with First World countries.
E – Improves the environmental factors of the economy.

Answer [   ]

12. The Use of 'Smacking'

As a teacher for nearly 20 years, I have never encountered an incident where it would have been acceptable for me to physically punish a child. I have around 25 pupils in each of my classes, and controlling them is no issue. Therefore I find it baffling that parents who deal with 2, 3 or 4 children, need to resort to physical means of punishment.

Whilst corporal punishment is regularly assessed and updated, it still remains acceptable for a parent or guardian to use 'smacking' as a way of chastising their children. Yet, there are no clear legalities surrounding this issue. The idea that smacking is acceptable, is quite frankly wrong, and highly unethical.

I find it remarkable how there seems to be more safety nets for adults than there are for children in regards to abuse, violence and physical behaviour. For adults, there are already multiple laws in place that include: violence against women, family violence prevention, crime and disorder, and domestic violence. It is extremely peculiar that there are such a lack of laws which protect children from violent punishments.

There has been building pressure to change the law in regards to how firmly a parent should be allowed to discipline their child. Organisations have become more focused on campaigns that highlight the need for a complete ban on smacking, to dispute the idea that physical punishment is acceptable.

Not only does smacking a child set a bad example in regards to behaviour, but it also demonstrates a poor way of dealing with different emotions. It teaches children that smacking is 'acceptable', and therefore they will be more inclined to act out in the same way.

It is quite obvious that smacking a child has visual side effects that are likely to cause some issues in the future. Using smacking as a form of punishment is likely to have psychological, attitudinal and social complications. A child may be encouraged to lie or hide their feelings if they know that being honest will get them smacked. They may become bitter, resentful and even angry towards other people as a defence mechanism.

There are other ways which should be used to punish a child. There is absolute no need to use any form of physical punishment, which will only make matters worse. Smacking will not resolve the situation on a long-term basis. Although it might fix the issue for a short-period of time, a child will learn to grow up with this behaviour as being the 'norm', and therefore this is likely to affect their development process.

Immediate action needs to be taken to completely ban so-called 'reasonable punishments'. It is not necessary, highly unethical and teaches a child to grow up using the same means of punishment that will continue to negatively impact society.

Question 40

Following on from the passage, what hypothetical conclusion would be *most* logical?

A – If parents continue to punish their child using smacking, the child will grow up hating them.

B – If physical punishments continue, then child cruelty is more likely to increase.

C – If child cruelty increases, the Government will be faced with issues that suggest they could have prevented it.

D – If a child acts out, that child needs to be punished.

E – If smacking is legal, it should be used.

Answer

Question 41

The use of the word "chastisement" can be *defined* as...

A – A minor error.

B – A small sentence.

C – A strong reprimand.

D – A price to pay.

E – An insignificant mishap.

Answer

Question 42

In paragraph one, what is the reasoning behind the author's negativity towards physical punishment?

A – She can control a class of up to 25 pupils without using physical punishment, so therefore parents who are dealing with smaller numbers of children can do the same.

B - She believes that physical punishment is cruel.

C – She would like to use physical punishments but can't do so as it is against the school rules.

D – She believes that it is a parent's responsibility to hand out punishments, not hers.

E – She was beaten as a child.

Answer

ANSWERS TO MULTIPLE-CHOICE – SECTION 2

'The Future of Education'

Q1. B = 'Address both sides of the argument, before forming a conclusion'.

EXPLANATION = the author uses the phrase "to look at both sides of the coin" in order to "address both sides of the argument, before forming a conclusion". The author demonstrates how all of the pros and cons need to be weighed up in order to assess the overall argument. It is important to distinguish two sides of an argument before reaching a plausible inference, yet from the passage it is clear that the author dismisses one side of the argument, in order to make their argument more assertive.

Q2. D = 'Children are becoming too reliant on technology'.

EXPLANATION = the author implies, but does not state, that "children are becoming too reliant on technology". The author discusses how children have become somewhat 'fixated' with the ideas of new technology, and the fact that they are growing up in a world full of advancing technology, means that they will be more inclined to use this for educational purposes, rather than old-fashioned textbooks.

Q3. D = 'Technology plays a vital role in producing incorrect or misleading information'.

EXPLANATION = the idea of a "dumbing down" society is used to highlight how "technology plays a vital role in producing incorrect or misleading information". The author suggests children are becoming more "dumb" because of the access to online information, that isn't always correct. The author goes on to discuss how children can struggle to differentiate credible sources from those less unreliable.

Q4. E = 'Incredulous'.

EXPLANATION = the authors tone of voice regarding technology in education can best be described as "incredulous". The author presents an argument that is quite sceptical and disapproving of the use of technology in educational institutions.

'Obesity and Culture'

Q5. E = 'Irony'.

EXPLANATION = the author uses irony with the intention of highlighting how the image that is constantly portrayed, doesn't reflect society.

Q6. C = 'Psychological problems are the underlying factor of obesity'.

EXPLANATION = the underlying assumption that can be made from the fourth paragraph is that "psychological problems are the underlying factor of obesity". The author refers to unpleasant experiences, and mental instabilities, which contribute to psychological issues which may result in obesity. It is also fair to assume that other lesser mental issues such as laziness, can be defined as 'psychological problems'.

Q7. C = 'The author highlights how obesity should not be considered a disability'.

EXPLANATION = the author has written the word *"actually"* in italics, in order to "highlight the authors ideas of how obesity should not be considered a disability". The author discusses how obesity is a preventable factor, and therefore lifestyles can be altered to improve a person's health. Therefore the author is suggesting that because obesity can be prevented, it should not be considered a form of disability.

Q8. B = 'Colloquialism'.

EXPLANATION = within the last paragraph, the author uses the term "couch potato" as a form of "colloquialism". Colloquialism is a technique where ordinary or familiar everyday phrases are used instead of formal or literary phrases.

'Natural Laws'

Q9. B = 'Ambiguous'.

EXPLANATION = the term "natural law" is implied to be "ambiguous". The term offers many theories and interpretations that make it difficult to fully comprehend. It is vague and unclear, and lacks substantial obtrusions that makes it difficult to define.

Q10. C = 'Inflexible and punitive'.

EXPLANATION = the author conveys that the use of the word "law" in context of "natural laws" is somewhat "inflexible and punitive". It relies on fixed ideas that makes is difficult to differentiate between different theories and understandings of the concept.

Q11. D = 'Philosophical'.

EXPLANATION = according to the passage, the author refers to natural laws in a "philosophical" approach. The natures of law are based upon philosophical ideas regarding ethics that form non-logical necessities of truth and actuality.

'Covering Disasters'

Q12. C = 'Europe judges international events based on the number of Europeans affected'.

EXPLANATION = the main assumption that can be made from the first passage is that "Europe judges the international events based on the number of Europeans affected". This assumption can be made based on the way the author describes how nations frame their coverage in association with who is affected.

Q13. D = 'The relationship between cause and effect'.

EXPLANATION = in paragraph four, the author uses the term "reflexivity" in order to demonstrate "the relationship between cause and effect". It demonstrates the relationship journalism has with events such as natural disasters, and how natural disasters impact the way in which journalism is conducted.

Q14. B = 'To highlight the authors interpretation of evidence lacking credibility and sincerity'.

EXPLANATION = the author addresses the term "evidence" by using inverted commas in order "to highlight the authors interpretation of the word, and how it can be seen to lack credibility and sincerity". The passage clearly indicates how news mediums are subjective and therefore interprets social events in a particular way, thus jeopardising the hidden truths of the actuality of the event.

Q15. B = 'The media act as a 'looking glass' to help society engage with social events from around the world'.

EXPLANATION = we are clearly shown how we, as the public, are given a window or "looking glass" via journalistic mediums, in order to help us understand what is going on.

'Same-Sex Marriage and Society'

Q16. C = 'Childish, immature, ignorant'.

EXPLANATION = the words "childish, immature and ignorant" are the best words to describe the comparison between current attitudes to gay people, and the behaviour commonly seen in a playground. The passage implies that gay people are singled out as 'being different' and are constantly having to defend themselves against childish, ignorant behaviour.

Q17. D = 'The sacred writings of religious views'.

EXPLANATION = the term 'scripture', in the context of the fifth passage refers to "sacred religious writings of religious views" such as the Bible or the Quran.

Q18. C = 'Some people continue to have doubts about gay marriage'.

EXPLANATION = the main assumption which can be made from the second paragraph is that "some people continue to have doubts about gay marriage". The passage indicates that although many people have softened their view towards gay marriage, some people still have their reservations.

'Doping in Sports'

Q19. E = 'Doping threatens the overall integrity of the sport'.

EXPLANATION = the main argument in which the author makes is that "doping threatens the overall integrity of the sport". The passage focuses primarily on perception and opinion on how sport is portrayed to the public. The author demonstrates the implications of doping through sporting activities, and how this negatively effects the reputation of sport in general.

Q20. D = 'Reputation'.

EXPLANATION = from reading the main passage, we can infer that the author strongly believes reputation to be incredibly important to the nature of sport. Sport focuses heavily on how athletes are perceived by the public; and therefore it needs to maintain a positive reputation, that isn't soiled by doping.

Q21. A = 'Unethical'.

EXPLANATION = the best word that describes the term 'doping' is "unethical". The author clearly highlights how doping is unfair on athletes who play by the rules. Doping is described as a form of cheating that ultimately gives an edge to athletes who take drugs to further improve their performance.

'Medical Marijuana'

Q22. B = 'Emphatic'.

EXPLANATION = the word that best describes the author's tone throughout the passage is emphatic. Emphatic can be defined as expressing something forcibly and clearly.

Q23. C = 'Put the readers in a position of someone else's shoes'.

EXPLANATION = the author uses a first person approach in order to put the reader in a position of unfamiliarity and engage with ideas that are felt by somebody else. The author uses this approach in order to engage the reader with the situation and make them feel as though they are experiencing it for themselves.

Q24. C = 'Marijuana is accepted as a form of medication in some places'.

EXPLANATION = the passage infers, but is not stated, that "marijuana is accepted as a form of medication in some places". Within the first passage, the author states how "all people with 'real' illnesses should be allowed to take marijuana as a form of medication, or at least, all be given the rights of choice". Therefore, this suggests that some places already use marijuana as a medical intervention.

Q25. C = 'Personal involvement'.

EXPLANATION = the main flaw of this argument is that it relies on "personal involvement" and opinions. The passage is written in first person, and therefore provides a personal account of the views of marijuana for medical use. The fact that the argument is based on personal experience and opinion doesn't provide a strong argument overall, therefore makes it flawed.

'Universities and Higher Paying Job Offers'

Q26. B = 'Attending a prestigious university allows graduates to earn more because of the university status'.

EXPLANATION = from author A's passage, the assumption that can be made from this argument is that "attending a prestigious university allows graduates to earn more because of the university status". The argument indicates that a degree from a prestigious university such as Oxford or Cambridge will give students a better chance of gaining better jobs, than those who attended lower ranked universities.

Q27. E = 'If students work hard, they should receive the benefits'.

EXPLANATION = the hypothetical reasoning from passage two, is "if students work hard, they should receive the benefits". A hypothetical reasoning can be illustrated by 'if this...then this'.

Q28. A = 'Students are lingering in education because of uncertainties regarding future careers'.

EXPLANATION = the use of the term "hanging out" in the context of author C's passage, is used to suggest that "students are lingering in education because of uncertainty regarding their future careers'. The author believes that students feel obligated to stay in education because the future of their career is uncertain. The passage clearly indicates how difficult it has become for the younger generation to gain employment.

'Legal Highs'

Q29. B = 'The uncertain health implications of legal highs, combined with their accessibility, presents a major challenge and risk to the public's health'.

EXPLANATION = the main conclusion from the passage is that "the uncertain health implications of illegal highs, combined with their accessibility, presents a major challenge and risk to the public's health". The author demonstrates the implications of taking legal highs and how the consequences of the consumption of such substances, can have a profound affect on a person. The author clearly emphasises how there is no scientific evidence to determine the risks involved with taking these substances, and therefore this poses a major health risk.

Q30. E = 'Alarmed'.

EXPLANATION = the tone of voice which the author uses when describing the implications of the term 'legal highs' is "alarmed". The author demonstrates how the term 'legal highs' is misleading and wrong, and discusses the problem of marketing these substances with a name that is so 'off-the-mark'.

Q31. D = 'How these substances can cause changes in brain function, which result in altered perception, attitude and behaviour.'

EXPLANATION = the use of the term "psychoactive substances" is used to illustrate "how these substances can cause changes in brain function, which result in altered perception, attitude and behaviour." The author demonstrates examples of the consequences of consuming legal highs, which are linked with brain function and the inability to control one's mind and state of well-being.

Q32. E = 'People should not be treated for self-inflicted issues'.

EXPLANATION = the conclusion that people using legal highs and illegal drugs, can be supported by the reasoning that suggests 'people should not be treated for self-inflicted issues.' The author addresses this issue in terms of choice and lifestyle.

'Combat Sport'

Q33. E = 'There is something to defend from'.

EXPLANATION = in paragraph three, the underlying assumption being made that 'even young girls are being taught to defend themselves from an early age' suggests "there is something that needs to be defended". The author uses the above sentence as a way of stating how society is 'preparing' children, even girls, to be equipped with knowledge and techniques in order to defend themselves, suggesting that, quite possibly, they will need to be able to defend themselves in some way or another.

Q34. A = 'The aims of the sport'.

EXPLANATION = the biggest difference between combat sport and 'less aggressive sports' is in "the aim of the sport". In 'less aggressive sport' such as football or rugby, the aim of the sport is to win the game by scoring goals or points. Injury is an unfortunate part of these sports, which is a result of unplanned conflict. In combat sport the main aim is to attack your opponent through fighting techniques. The only way you can win is to subdue your opponent until they are physically unable to continue, or surrender.

Q35. D = 'Rhetorical Questioning'.

EXPLANATION = the literary technique that is used here, is rhetorical questioning. A rhetorical question is a figure of speech in the form of a question, which is used to emphasise a point, rather than generate an answer to the question. The writer here is trying to make the point that children who are 'taught to fight to protect themselves from losing' will quickly lose the ability to distinguish between using these skills in the sport based environment, and in the real world.

Q36. C = 'An analogy'.

EXPLANATION = in order to compare combat sports with 'less aggressive sports' the author uses "an analogy" in order to make the connection. An analogy helps to establish a relationship based on similarities of two conceptual ideas. The analogy is used to counter the argument that combat sports are no different to less aggressive sports such as football.

'Tourism in the Developing World'

Q37. E = 'Author E'.

EXPLANATION = the author that highlights the importance of possible Government intervention is "author E". Author E discusses higher powers that are likely to get involved in order to generate and encourage tourism. No other author refers to any form of higher power or government intervention.

Q38. D = 'The tourism industry has helped transform societies for the worst'.

EXPLANATION = in author D's paragraph, the main conclusion that can be inferred is that "the tourism industry has helped transform societies for the worst". The author discusses examples where tourism has helped and worsen the lives of people living in negative circumstances.

Q39. B = 'Improves the social infrastructures of society'.

EXPLANATION = the underlying assumption in which tourism is supposed to generate can be concluded as "improv[ing] the social infrastructures of society". All of the authors discuss the importance of tourism by improving the foundations of their society. The infrastructures is what builds the foundations of a society and therefore these need to be improved in order to improve the lives of Third World civilians.

'The Use of Smacking'

Q40. B = 'If physical punishments continue, then child cruelty is more likely to increase'.

EXPLANATION = following on from the passage, the hypothetical reasoning that would be most logical is "if physical punishments continue, then child cruelty is more likely to increase". The author highlights the implications of using smacking as a means of punishment, and suggests that it is likely to cause issues for the future which result in an increase in child cruelty.

Q41. C = 'A strong reprimand'.

EXPLANATION = the use of the word "chastisement" in the context of the passage is used to demonstrate "a strong reprimand". The author highlights the importance of punishing a child in the correct way without the need of smacking.

Q42. A = 'She can control a class of up to 25 pupils without using physical punishment, so therefore parents who are dealing with smaller numbers of children can do the same'.

EXPLANATION = The reasoning behind the author's negativity towards physical punishment is due to the fact that "she can control a class of up to 25 pupils without using physical punishment, so therefore parents who are dealing with smaller numbers of children can do the same". This is made clear by the way the author compares her situation with those parents.

SAMPLE ESSAY QUESTIONS

SECTION B

Answer **one** of the following questions.

Your answer should be a reasoned and substantiated argument, which justifies your response to the question that you have chosen.

1. "Arranged marriages should no longer be tolerated within Western societies". Discuss.

2. Should abortions be made illegal for everyone?

3. Does home-schooling damage children's social skills?

HOW TO ANSWER THE QUESTIONS

For Section B, you will be required to answer only **one** question out of three possible choices.

Your answer should be no longer than 750 words, and a standard essay should be between 500 to 600 words. You will only have 40 minutes to conduct the entire essay, and so time management is crucial.

You will need to construct a clear and concise argument that is straight to the point, provides a quality argument, and most importantly, is written in a persuasive, controlled and detailed structure.

Understanding the Question

As mentioned in Chapter 1, the LNAT does not require high levels of knowledge, and is not a test which you can study for.

The best preparation for your LNAT in regards to the essay section of the assessment, is to practice drafting essay plans and reading high quality newspapers (usually in the form of a broadsheet). Reading newspapers will allow you to gain a basic understanding of the goings-on in the world around you, including current affairs, economics, technological changes, and social developments.

You are not expected to have a detailed understanding of the essay topics which will appear in the exam. What is expected from you, is to create an argument based on explanations, assumptions and analysis that fundamentally form a persuasive and conclusive argument.

Essay Topic

When choosing which question you are going to answer, it is important that you feel comfortable enough to write approximately 600 words on that topic in a clear, informative and analytical manner.

You will need to keep yourself informed of current affairs and read up on what is going on both internationally and locally, if you wish to score high marks on your LNAT.

We advise that you pick a topic in which you feel knowledgeable enough to produce a definitive for or against argument, i.e. are you for or against the claim? Do you agree or disagree with the question?

Structure of the Essay

You need to have the ability to coherently structure your argument so that it reads correctly. The sole purpose of the LNAT essay is for you to demonstrate your ability and skill to persuasively conduct an argument and convey your thoughts in the best light possible.

Although your essay **does not** get marked, and **it does not** form part of your LNAT score, it will be the **only** piece of writing that your chosen university will have access to. If your multiple-choice grade is borderline, then it is likely that your university will make their decision based upon your answers to the essay section. Therefore it is very important that you are prepared for this section.

During the planning stages of your essay, you should ask yourself the following four questions:

WHAT? *What* is the motion being put forward? Is the question based on politics, economics, ethics or something else? *What* is the question exactly asking of you? You will need to demonstrate high levels of critical awareness and determine what the question is asking, before attempting to answer it.

WHY? *Why* is the question being asked? *Why* is it significant? What might the evidence be to suggest it is accurate/inaccurate? What is the purpose of the proposed statement? *Why* is the question being challenged? *Why* use certain terms, phrases or literary techniques? This section requires your analytical ability and the skill to be persuasive.

HOW? *How* is this statement concluded? What are the practicalities of enforcing this statement? *How* can this be challenged? *How* can this be enforced? *How* can this be monitored? You will need to demonstrate how your answer forms a solid conclusion based on the reasoning that you have provided.

3

WHAT IF? *What* are the alternatives? Are there any other views to consider? What are the practical implications of the argument? How can these be challenged? What are the strengths and weaknesses of both sides of the argument?

4

The structure of your essay is important. You need to be able to convey each stage of your thought process. You will likely have had to write lots of essays prior to taking your LNAT assessment. Thus, you will be no stranger to the basic format of any essay: the *introduction*, the *main body* and the *conclusion*. This is no different in the LNAT.

STRUCTURE OF YOUR ESSAY

INTRODUCTION. The introduction will be the first thing that the reader will look at, and so it is important to give a clear and concise overview of what your essay is going to be about.

Your introduction should include the purpose of the essay, what your initial thoughts may be, what you hope to achieve/find, enumerate the points you wish to make, and define the overall importance of your argument and why it is relevant/significant.

MAIN BODY. During the main body of your essay, you should remember to keep in mind the questions mentioned previously in regards to *what, why, how* and *what if.*

You need to make points and back them up using examples and evidence in order to strengthen your overall argument. There is no point making a statement, if you have nothing to back up the reasoning for it. Your argument needs to be straight to the point, persuasive and significant to illustrate what you are trying to say.

Usually, 3-4 high quality points is enough to make a good argument. Do not waffle. Expand on a few points and provide analysis and detail, as opposed to briefly mentioning lots of points and not going into enough detail about each of them. Your essay needs to read coherently.

CONCLUSION. Your conclusion should summarise your whole argument. It is often said that a reader should be able to read an introduction and a conclusion, and still have a basic understanding of what your argument is about.

Your conclusion should not introduce any new points, and should only sum up the points that you have written about previously.

The conclusion should be short, to the point and significant. If you can summarise your argument using three to four sentences, your reader will be impressed and know what you were trying to achieve.

Make sure that your conclusion refers back to the question you were given. Make sure that the question has been answered directly, and demonstrate where you stand on the subject matter.

SAMPLE QUESTIONS – ANSWERS

Question 1

'Arranged marriages should no longer be tolerated within Western societies'. Discuss.

This question focuses on your ability to discuss opinions and provide valuable explanations and examples, in order to *discuss* the importance of both sides of the argument.

To argue **'for'** banning arranged marriages, the key points you could include are:

- As human beings, it is in our nature to find our own life partner through freedom of choice. You could expand on this claim by providing examples of freedom of choice, equality and diversity;

- It can be argued that arranged marriages can lead to abuse, neglect and deprivation that could have been avoided if a person was given the opportunity to make their own choices;

- Arranged marriage is a barrier to integration. It encourages segregation and rejects diversity and equality. You could talk about different cultures and how in some cultures, this is deemed to be the 'norm' and therefore prolongs their culture to live through exclusion and repression;

- Arranged marriages are not theologically supported by any religion. It has no place in society. You can talk about how societies are evolving and adapting in order to maintain an effective society, and therefore arranged marriages have become somewhat 'outdated' and 'old-fashioned';

- You could discuss how on a subconscious level, arranged marriages are used as a way of controlling a person by arranging the marriage, despite what the man and woman want;

- Banning arranged marriages will allow women to feel more in control, confident and equal. Women will be given the choice of choosing their life partner and this illustrates how times have changed, and how women are becoming more in control of their own lives.

To argue **'against'** arranged marriages, the key points that you could include are:

- Religions and customs are difficult to separate and would prove extremely difficult to change. You can discuss how arranged marriages are more apparent in some cultures than in others, and highlight the implications of removing traditions from a culture that have ultimately been followed for hundreds of years;

- Perception of cultural attack. The perception of attacking a person's beliefs and culture could be seen as discriminatory. People will feel victimised and disassociated with wider cultures. You can discuss how societies have become notoriously aware of equality and discrimination. Attacking a person's culture and their traditions could be seen to be an act of discrimination, which will ultimately cause conflict amongst cultures, religions and society;

- Taking away a person's traditions. It may be tradition for arranged marriages to take place, and taking it away from their culture, is taking away what they believe in. From generations to generations, it is likely that family members have been subject to arranged marriages, because family history has been no different;

- Outlawing arranged marriages would violate people's civil rights and family values;

- People are not *forced* to have an arranged marriage. There is a huge difference between arranged marriage and forced marriage. You could discuss this further and demonstrate examples for why arranged marriages should not be outlawed because the participants are not forced to go through with the marriage.

Question 2

Should abortions be made illegal for everyone?

This question focuses on your ability to discuss your opinions and provide valuable explanations and examples as to why you have chosen your argument.

To argue **'for'** making abortions illegal to everyone, the key points you could include are:

- Morally wrong. You could discuss the importance of morals and how it can be deemed morally wrong in society. You could talk about 'murder' and how this is deemed unacceptable;

- You could focus on the belief that an unborn child has the right to life. The baby did not ask to be brought into this world, and yet should be able to live regardless;

- You could discuss how many people believe that the unborn child is already considered alive whilst forming in the foetus;

- You could discuss how many campaigns have been instigated to illustrate that after conceiving, a baby is automatically growing and therefore has its own life;

- Everyone should be able to have the same rights, and so it is unfair for some people to be allowed to have an abortion, where in other cultures it is not acceptable;

- There are alternative methods of giving up your baby instead of abortions, such as adoption. You could discuss how abortions are considered a violent act, and there are other ways to settle having a child, despite not wanting it. These options allow people who cannot have a child to be given the opportunity to get one through adoption etc.

To argue **'against'** making abortions illegal for everyone, the key points you could include are:

- You could argue that it is someone's body, and therefore it is their choice as to whether or not they want to keep the baby. A person's body, a person's choice. They are in charge of what goes on with their body and how they wish to proceed. If they wish to terminate their pregnancy, then human rights should allow this to happen;

- Circumstances. You could argue that certain circumstances, such as rape would make someone want to have an abortion. You could argue the extent to which rape, and other forms of sexual abuse are not uncommon, and therefore are likely to have a huge impact on whether a mother wants to keep their unborn child;

- The belief that the unborn child is just an embryo and is 'not alive'. Some people believe that the unborn child is not alive at the time of conception, and therefore there is still time to terminate the pregnancy without causing any pain or harm to the foetus;

- Foetuses are incapable of feeling pain when abortions are performed. You can argue that if the baby is not alive, and feels no pain when a termination is being conducted, there is no reason why a woman should not be given the choice of terminating her pregnancy;

- Modern abortion procedures are safe and do not cause lasting health issues;

- The right to freedom of choice. This is a huge debate which you could discuss in lengthy detail. As humans, we are all granted the same human rights, and therefore you argue how a woman should be given the same right to decide whether to proceed with her pregnancy;

- Abortions give the woman the choice of terminating a pregnancy if they find abnormalities in the foetus. A mother is able to terminate her pregnancy if she knows the baby is going to have severe abnormalities that will ultimately affect the lifestyle of the baby. This can be considered as having the unborn child's 'best interests' at heart;

- A baby should not come into the world unwanted and therefore women should be given the right to end their pregnancy if they want to do so.

Question 3

Does home-schooling damage children's social skills?

This question requires you to adopt a view either **for** or **against** home-schooling, and whether you believe it damages children's social skills.

To argue **'for'** home-schooling damaging children's social skills, the key points you could include are:

- Children need to be able to engage with social surroundings in order to experience certain social situations. You could argue how child development is important for a child from an early age, and should therefore experience the same level of social activity as every other child;

- Not being properly socialised can lead to shyness, being sheltered from the rest of the world, and anxious and timid behaviour when it comes to engaging in social situations in the future. Ultimately, home-schooling could have long-lasting effects which will affect the way in which that child grows up and interacts when it comes to finding employment, meeting new friends and having relationships;

- Age is an extremely important point to consider in relation to socialisation. Children are still learning the expectations and norms of society, and thus would not be able to engage with current social norms if they were to be home- schooled. They would not be engaging with other children of their age, nor would they be experiencing the same level of education as other children who attend school;

- Child development is a crucial stage when it comes to learning and interacting with social surroundings. Being home-schooled takes this away. You could discuss how many theories have been undertaken in regards to child development and social activity. The majority of theorists suggest that children need consistent levels of activity and social interaction in order to maintain a stable and healthy development level.

To argue **'against'** home-schooling damaging children's social skills, the key points you could include are:

- You could write about how children in schools can be just as shy and reserved as home-schooled children. You could use examples to explain how children who attend schools can be just as anxious and sheltered from social interactions, and vice versa. Children who are home-schooled could be active, friendly and interact with others, and children who go to school can still be shy and awkward. Social development is different for every child, regardless of their surroundings;

- Education does not spend a great deal of time teaching social skills. Thus, children who are home-schooled can experience the same level of social interaction as children who do attend a school. Social skills are qualities that can be taught outside the classroom, where children are more likely to engage with each other at home or in a park, as opposed to on the school grounds;

- Social skills can be taught from home. Parents can develop their children's social interaction by engaging them in certain social activities. People who spend time nurturing their children, and improve their children's learning and social interaction, are far more likely to see higher results. This is in contrast to parents who send their child to school with little knowledge of the friendships they've made, or how actively involved their child is with other pupils.

ESSAY
(SECTION 1)

SECTION B OF THE LNAT) – ESSAY QUESTION

Answer **one** of the following questions.

Your answer should be a reasoned and substantiated argument, which justifies your response to the question that you have chosen.

You have 40 minutes in which to draft and write your answer to one essay question.

1. Discuss the justification of using Military Force.

2. In what circumstances is abortion socially acceptable?

3. Should animals be born and kept in captivity?

We have provided you with space to write out an answer or draft to the questions above. Additional paper may be required.

1. Discuss the justification of using Military Force.

2. In what circumstances is abortion socially acceptable?

3. Should animals be born and kept in captivity?

ANSWERS TO ESSAY QUESTIONS (SECTION 1)

1. Discuss the justification of using Military Force.

For this question, it is important that you fully comprehend the word *"justification"*. In other words, can the use of Military Force ever be justified? Can it be reasoned? Are there certain circumstances that should allow the Military to get involved? The use of the word discuss means that the examiner is looking for you to weigh up the pros and cons of using the Military, and from that, illustrate your own opinions.

Below are some of the key points that you could include in order to strengthen your answer and provide a successful response.

Define. The first part of your essay should include an introduction regarding the Military Forces, the role which they play within society, and what you aim to discuss and establish. You could also include probable hypothesis and assumptions which you think you might find. If you do include assumptions, you need to make sure that these are clearly answered in your essay.

Defence. You need to come up with situations that could or should require the use of the Armed Forces. The most obvious answer for justification of using the Military is a defence mechanism. If a country is under attack from another country, that country should be able to have the right to defend themselves and protect themselves. The Military provides a professional way to deal with matters that are ultimately out of the hands of society.

State interests. You could argue that the Military have the right to get involved when rival powers threaten the security and national interests of the state, in a way which justifies a military response.

Military force vs. proliferation of weapons of mass destruction. You need to be able to distinguish between military force and weapons of mass destruction. Using military force is justifiable when you think of how much it prevents the proliferation of weapons of mass destruction. The damage caused by military force is far less than the potential damage caused by the use of weapons of mass destruction. Military force aims to defend its citizens and nation from outside threats, and therefore this is reason enough for the military to be involved in situations that require attention, but do not require destruction.

Counter-argument 1. The question requires you to discuss this topic, and therefore requires you to give both the good and bad points about using the Military. You could counter-argue the above points by demonstrating that a situation does not necessarily require a full scale military attack. Sometimes, there are other ways of resolving a situation, which should be considered first, before making the decision to get politically involved and ultimately causing further disputes.

Counter-argument 2. The use of military force can be sometimes be taken more irrationally than anticipated. Once the Military becomes involved, it automatically escalates the situation. The Military are a sign of government involvement, and therefore sends a particular message.

Opinion. You need to demonstrate your view on the topic and where you stand in regards to the justification of using military force. Try including examples or possible scenarios in order to strengthen your argument, and make valid assertions. It is important that you fully answer all parts of the question, as well as providing as much evidence and analysis as possible, to ensure higher marks.

2. In what circumstances is abortion socially acceptable?

For this question, you should discuss the pros and cons of abortion. You can assume from the question that there are circumstances in which you can argue abortion is socially acceptable. However, if you have strong views and believe that there are no circumstances that allow this to be acceptable, you can challenge this question as long as you provide clear examples, reasoning and analysis as to why you have come to this conclusion.

Below are some of the key points that you could include in order to strengthen your answer and provide a successful response.

Define 'Socially Acceptable'. First of all, you need to have a general understanding of what is meant by the term 'socially acceptable'. Offer a definition of socially acceptable that could be along the lines of: socially acceptable is a term used to highlight what is generally acceptable by the mainstream population. You could also argue that social acceptability can vary depending on the different values, beliefs, religions and traditions which people have on particular topics.

Circumstance 1. You could argue that abortions are socially acceptable if a woman has been impregnated without her consent. This argument considers rape, where the woman was in a situation that she could not control, and was dominated by another person. In these types of cases, abortion is often considered socially acceptable because the woman did not choose to become pregnant and was forced into sexual relations. You could argue how a woman would not want a constant reminder of what she went through, and should not have to raise a child belonging to a man of that sort.

Circumstance 2. Some cultures have made it legal for women to have an abortion, and this demonstrates how abortions have become socially acceptable. Culture plays a significant role in our values and beliefs, and thus if it has been deemed *culturally* acceptable, then it must be *socially* acceptable.

Counter-argument 1. You could follow the above circumstance with a counter-argument and illustrate how in some cultures, it is still illegal to have an abortion. Despite this, some women of that culture still choose to have an abortion, despite it being illegal. Some of them do this in extremely unpleasant ways.

Circumstance 3. Some women may choose to have an abortion due to personal circumstances. For example, if a woman, or girl gets pregnant at an early age. In contemporary society, we are seeing more and more young girls having children. The fact that they are still children themselves means that they often lack the resources to adequately look after a new-born baby, and therefore may wish to have an abortion because it is 'not the right time.'

Circumstance 4. Sometimes, a woman may need to have an abortion for medical reasons. This is not the fault of the woman, and therefore cannot be controlled. If continuing with the pregnancy puts the woman's life in jeopardy, then abortion is the best option, in order to protect the life of the woman.

Counter-argument 2. Many people believe that even an unborn baby has the right to life. Many people argue that human life begins at conception and therefore an unborn baby is already considered alive. The term abortion is a controversial issue in lots of different cultures, and some people consider them to be morally wrong.

Examples. Try to think of examples to support your reasoning. For example, you can use the example of a person living an unhealthy lifestyle i.e. drugs and alcohol, and demonstrate how this person would not be seen as 'fit' to bring a child into the world.

3. Should animals be born and kept in captivity?

This question solely relies on your personal opinion. You need to decide whether you believe animals should be born and kept in captivity, or whether you are against this. In order for you to gain high marks in this question, you will need to have a solid understanding of the term *captivity*. You need to be able to weigh up the pros and cons and determine your own personal belief based on persuasive, intellectual and analytical reasoning.

Below are some of the key points that you could include in order to strengthen your answer and provide a successful response.

Entertainment. One reason you could use to argue for animals being born and kept in captivity, is that research has shown that animals are increasingly popular with humans. They provide great entertainment for zoos and aquariums, where they are nurtured and raised so that they develop in an environment that is not threatened by poachers or by the destruction of their habitat.

Counter-argument. You could argue against the above point, by indicating that whilst animals may provide entertainment value, they need to experience the correct growth and development process. Animals cannot be kept in zoos and expected to have the same skills and life as the same type of animal in the wild. Within captivity, animals experience small enclosed cages, they do not need to hunt for their food, they are raised by human interaction, and they are cared for in a way that makes them incapable of ever being nurtured for in the wild.

Keeps them safe. You could argue that another reason for animals to be born and kept in captivity is to reduce the risk and hazards that they may face in the wild. Animals face several threats whilst living in the wild. For example, deforestation, poaching, destruction of habitats and a lack of food are all examples of threats that captivity subsequently keeps them at bay from. Animals do not have to worry about being in captivity due to them being well looked after.

Counter-argument 2. It can be considered morally wrong to choose the fate of an animal. An animal should have the same rights to live as we do. If someone tried putting a human in a cage, and kept them locked up from the rest of society, this would automatically be considered wrong. Why is it different for animals?

Counter-argument 3. It is not their natural habitat. Being born and growing up in captivity is not a solid ground for nurturing and development. The animal experiences the opposite to what they would in their natural habitat. They become more reliant on humans, and therefore are unable to defend for themselves.

Opinion. This type of question relies heavily on your opinion and how well you are able to support your reasons for your belief. You need to engage the reader with clear, concise and persuasive reasoning and examples in order to gain high marks. Conveying your opinion shows the examiner your ability to form a conclusion, based on the argument you provide. Examiners do not like to see candidate's responses that 'sit on the fence' and weigh up both the good and bad options. Yes, it is important that you are able to demonstrate critical analysis of both sides, but you can take your argument further by highlighting your views. This will give your argument a personal element, which demonstrates how much you have engaged with the topic.

ESSAY
(SECTION 2)

SECTION B OF THE LNAT) – ESSAY QUESTION

Answer **one** of the following questions.

Your answer should be a reasoned and substantiated argument, which justifies your response to the question that you have chosen.

You have 40 minutes in which to draft and write your answer to one essay question.

1. "Euthanasia should be legal". Discuss.

2. Should the death penalty be allowed?

3. "Violent games contribute to youth violence". Argue.

We have provided you with space to write out an answer or draft to the questions above. Additional paper may be required.

1. "Euthanasia should be legal". Discuss.

2. Should the death penalty be allowed?

3. "Violent games contribute to youth violence". Argue.

ANSWERS TO ESSAY QUESTIONS (SECTION 2)

1. "Euthanasia should be legal". Discuss.

For this type of question, you need to have a solid understanding of the term "euthanasia". You need to have enough knowledge regarding this concept in order to make a persuasive argument for or against it being legalised. It is important that you provide clear reasoning for your belief. To make your argument stronger, we suggest using counter-arguments, with the intention of disproving or dismissing these arguments in order to further your reasoning.

Below are some of the key points that you could include in order to strengthen your answer and provide a successful response.

Definition. You need to demonstrate a solid understanding of the term euthanasia. An important part of the essay is in your ability to distinguish whether or not euthanasia should be legalised, and therefore you need to understand the concept fully before deciding to argue one way or the other. Does an individual who has no hope for recovery, who is in a great deal of pain, have the right to decide how and when to end their life? Euthanasia is a term that refers to the act of killing by permitting the death of hopelessly sick or injured individuals. Assisted suicide is another term that is often linked with euthanasia.

Dignity. Within a civilized society, it can be argued that an individual should be able to die in a dignified and peaceful way, instead of waiting for a disease to kill them. Some people have become so inflicted with pain that it is too much to bare.

Bodies are our own. It can be argued that it is up to us to decide what we do with our bodies. Our bodies are our own. We are allowed to make all kinds of bodily decisions. For example, getting tattoos, piercings, having a baby, getting a transplant, getting plastic surgery etc, thus we should also be able to decide when our body has had enough.

Beliefs. Some people believe that suicide is not a crime. People commit suicide and no crime has been committed, and no one was in the wrong. Therefore, euthanasia should also not be a crime. The only difference between the two is that euthanasia usually requires the assistance of someone else.

The assisted help from someone willing to let a person die ultimately fulfils a dying person's wishes.

Changing attitudes. According to a study conducted in 2007, 80% of the public said that they wanted the law to change regarding assisted suicide and helping sufferers to end their life.

Counter-argument 1. Some people believe that life is ultimately given by God, and it is up to God when that life should be taken. Taking this power into their own hands effectively tampers with religion and some people's beliefs of what is right and wrong. Be careful when using this argument, as generally you'll need evidence to support your points.

Counter-argument 2. Another argument that you could make against euthanasia becoming legalised is the impact that this will have on our legal system. The existing laws in place that stop euthanasia from happening would be imposed upon, and might become abused. Legalised euthanasia could result in people being killed despite not really wanting to die.

Counter-argument 3. Another argument concerns the hypothetical boundaries of legalised assisted suicide. There is no clear distinction or definition on what constitutes a person as 'seriously ill', and leaving such a topic open to interpretation, would provide all kinds of issues.

Evidence. For this type of essay, it will be very difficult to provide statistics or evidence unless you have previously studied the topic. However, you can still use examples and fictional scenarios in order to strengthen your argument. This will demonstrate that you have thought logically about your reasoning, supported it with an example and emphasised your viewpoints in a strong and coherent manner.

2. Should the death penalty be allowed?

This type of question requires you to demonstrate your ability to make a persuasive argument either for or against the death penalty and whether it should be allowed. Within this essay, you will need to use reasoning, examples, analysis and persuasion in order to create an effective and persuasive written argument. Examiners are hoping to see compelling arguments, that don't just 'sit on the fence' with their responses. They want to see your opinions, and how you can support your argument through written techniques.

Below are some of the key points you could include in order to strengthen your answer and provide a successful response.

Definition. You should begin your essay by explaining what the term 'death penalty' means. The death penalty can be defined as a sentence or punishment of death by execution. The most serious of offences are the only crimes that result in the use of the death penalty. Crimes including murder, treason and espionage are some of the crimes that were previously considered *capital offences.*

Retribution. The idea of "an eye for an eye" demonstrates how if one life is taken by an individual, that individual should also have their life taken. Retribution is a way of gaining justice and honours the victim by consoling those closest to them, with the knowledge that justice has been done.

Law. Using the death penalty is an important means of preserving law and order. Not only will the use of the death penalty deter crimes, but it also costs less than if you were to imprison offenders.

Prevention. Using the death penalty for *capital offences* will ensure that perpetrators will not be given the opportunity to commit further tragedies. Unlike imprisonment, death penalties ensure that the individual pays for their mistakes and keeps society safe from further crimes. Imprisonment is unable to achieve this. Imprisonment only works for as long as that person remains in prison or jail. Once their sentence is finished, and they are released back into civilised society, they are given the opportunity to commit further crimes, especially if they hold no remorse for their previous actions.

Counter-argument 1. You could argue that imprisonment sentences are a more effective way of maintaining civilisation, and proving a point to the perpetrator. Life-long sentences are a long lasting and severe punishment that force the individual to think about his actions and the consequences involved. This is a more effective way of taking criminals out of society, without the need for death.

Counter-argument 2. The death penalty is a very serious punishment, which cannot be taken back or amended. If the outcome of a trial or court case is actually incorrect, then the defendant is being subjected to the ultimate unfair punishment of death.

Therefore, using other punishments such as long-term imprisonment can ultimately save the life of someone who has been falsely accused.

Counter-argument 3. Not only is the death penalty an expensive punishment to conduct, but the death penalty is an easy way out for perpetrators. Imprisoning criminals forces them to live a solitary life in prison, and gives them the chance to think about their actions and understand the importance of morals, attitude and behaviour.

Within this essay, it does not matter which view you decide to take in regards to whether you believe the death penalty should be allowed; what does matter is your strong reasoning and use of examples in order to support your argument. The examiner wants to see an essay that is full of insightful knowledge and understanding that can be used to persuasively argue a case for or against a particular topic.

3. "Violent games contribute to youth violence". Discuss.

Within the above question, you are given a cause (video games) and an affect (youth violence). For this essay, you need to use the cause in order to weigh up the affect it has on youth and whether this contributes to youth violence. You need to discuss the proponents and opponents in relation to this topic, in order to illustrate an informed argument that demonstrates your views on the subject matter.

Below are some of the key points that you could include in order to strengthen your answer and provide a successful response.

Controversial. This is a very controversial topic, and has been debated, researched and analysed by many. Within this essay, it is important that you highlight your views and use examples where possible. The fact that this topic is so controversial may help you to use counter-arguments in your essay; in order to emphasise a point that you are trying to make.

Increase in popularity. You could argue that violent games have become increasingly popular within contemporary society, and therefore play a huge role in the behaviour and attitudes of the younger generation. There have been an increased number of games relating to violence and shooting, and therefore you can discuss the affect that this has on the minds of the younger generation.

Moral panic. There has been a lot of panic in societies regarding the impact that violent video games are having on younger people. These games are often blamed for school shootings, aggressive behaviour, increased bullying and physical acts of violence.

'Hypodermic Needle' Theory. Some researchers have studied the relationship between the impacts of these games in relation to social theories such as social learning and hypodermic methods. The idea is that young people are *injected* with information contained within the games, and that their social learning of the real world is infiltrated by visions of destruction, anger and violence. Therefore, this can be seen as a contributing factor regarding youth violence in terms of the games that they play.

Media. The media have become concerned with the link between youth violence and the impact of video games. The media are predominantly concerned with the *enthusiastic gamer* who cannot differentiate between the fantasy world of gaming and the real world. It is often argued that young people are unable to separate the characters behaviour in a game, with their own behaviour in real life. The media often focus on the negative psychological ways that video games affect children, with users having little to no knowledge of what the games are teaching them.

Desensitisation. Critics often argue that violent games desensitise players to violence. This theory is used to highlight diminished emotional responsiveness to negative stimuli after repeated exposure. It is often used to indicate how children become effected by the messages and visual aids that they witness in violent games, and how they become somewhat immune to the portrayal of violent behaviour.

Counter-argument 1. There is no evidence to suggest that gamers are unable to distinguish between the gaming world and the real world, and therefore these concerns in relation to violent games being a contribution to violent youths can be overlooked.

Counter-argument 2. It could also be argued that violent games do not cause violent behaviour. However, what could be considered is the possibility that violent people seek out these types of games as a way of entertainment and adhering to their violent nature. This acts as a counter view to violence being the cause, and suggests that the actual cause of violent behaviour is an aggressive individual.

Counter-argument 3. Playing or watching violent images can be used to reduce the violent behaviour of young people, particularly in boys, by acting as a substitute for 'rough and tumble' play. These violent images act as a means of expression which allows children to express their aggression without causing physical harm.

Controversial. The topic is so heavily debated and disputed that it is impossible to form a solid conclusion on whether or not violent games *actually* have a profound effect on today's youth, and cause them to become more violent. Within this essay, you can only offer your opinion in regards to what you believe to be the truth, based on prior knowledge about the issue.

LNAT MOCK
TEST

During this chapter, we have provided you with a sample LNAT mock test, in order to provide you with a similar experience to the real thing.

What to expect

Your Law National Admissions Test is comprised of two sections: multiple-choice questions and an essay. You will be given 2 hours and 15 minutes to complete the assessment.

Remember!

After you have completed Section A of the exam, and move on to Section B, **you will not** be able to return to the first section of the exam.

Multiple-choice

- You will be given 95 minutes to answer 42 questions;

- You will be given 12 passages, in which you will need to answer 3 to 4 questions for each.

Essay question

- You will be given 40 minutes to plan and write your essay;

- For this section of the exam, you will be given a choice of 3 questions, of which you must answer 1.

You should use this sample mock test to familiarise yourself with the layout, conditions, time limits, and questions in which you will face during your LNAT assessment.

You have 2 hours and 15 minutes in which to complete the mock exam.

Good luck.

SECTION A – MULTIPLE-CHOICE

You have 95 minutes in which to read the 12 passages and answer all 42 questions.

1. Educational Science and Society

The use of science in education is used to provide a practical message to young people. However, the younger generation are finding it more and more difficult to apply the lessons that they have learned from their scientific education in the real world.

Society has changed considerably over time, and consequently, so has the world of science. In the first half of the 20th century, global wars meant that worldwide governments provided funds for their scientists to research technical and highly advanced wartime applications.

Science is never static; it changes and adapts to reflect sociological shifts. The use of science in education supposedly helps a child to comprehend the world in which we live. Children are expected to become acquainted with past and present scientific discoveries, and to understand the importance of logical, technical and scientific methodology. These expectations open up a range of problems. Children who were fortunate enough to attend good schooling will inevitably develop a wider knowledge than those who weren't, but does this really better prepare them for 'the real world'?

For examinations, children are expected not only to understand scientific methods and factual information, but to apply these methods in a testing situation. The problem with this is that children are being taught through learning methods that concentrate on memory and theoretical knowledge, rather than through active and direct learning. Even teachers are no better off when it comes to putting science into action, and have a very limited understanding of how their subject relates with the real world. As a result, taught science is rapidly descending into the realms of farce.

The way in which educated people respond to the notion that they should show a clear understanding of science, is seen as 'quackery'. The astrological and philosophical ideas surrounding science have produced no visible effect in regards to standardised knowledge. The best result we can realistically expect from taught science is that there will be a very small minority of people who have developed *some* knowledge of the techniques and methods needed to apply the subject in real life.

Personally, I find it hugely ironic that schools expect so much from their children, yet teachers and examination boards fail to see the importance of active and direct learning, instead of relying on instant memory and theoretical knowledge. Due to the way science is currently taught, it is practically impossible for children to understand and interact with the subject.

Question 1

Which of the following *best* describes the author's concerns about science?

A – A belief that no educated person possesses.

B – Acknowledgment of the failed idea of science.

C – The current teaching system is not supportive for students who want to learn about the subject.

D – The idea that science is not fully understood.

E – The belief that scientists share science as being the centre focus of the world around us.

Answer

Question 2

The author's attitude towards public and secondary school education in relation to science is…

A – Supportive.

B – Contemptuous.

C – Against.

D – Indifferent.

E – Belligerent.

Answer

Question 3

The author uses which of the following to blame the failures of scientific methods in relation to education? **Two** answers required.

A – Lack of interest by the students.
B – Lack of support by parents.
C – Lack of direct experience for children.
D – Lack of structure within the educational system.
E – Teaching methods.

Answer

Question 4

Which *one* of the following cannot be inferred from the passage?

A – Children who attend good schools will receive a better education than those who don't.
B – It is relatively simple to learn the methods of scientific discoveries.
C – Some science has embedded into children's knowledge.
D – There is more than one reason for the failure of teaching sciences.
E – The world of science probes wide debates and controversy.

Answer

2. The Decline of Different Languages

It has become apparent that over the years, languages have become a dying out concept, and society has let this happen. The decline of different languages is clearly linked with political and economic factors that continue to undermine the power of language, and the influence it creates within society.

Ultimately, we choose to develop or enhance the language system by applying an effect that will change the overall outcome; whether that outcome is good or not cannot be determined until the effects have taken place, and then it is too late to undo what has already been done.

British civilisation is decadent and our language has collapsed. We find it in ourselves to debate about the declining nature of languages and yet we remain inactive. We assume that these changes cannot be acted upon and follow the idea that languages struggle against sentimental archaism. Language is used in a variety of ways, and sometimes used incorrectly. These incorrect usages of language makes it even more complex to understand. There is a fine line between people who understand the correct use of language, and people who use language in a way that becomes socially acceptable.

A major influence on the decline of languages is through the educational system. Languages are not being taught like they used to be, and have become distanced from the education system. From my experience, fewer people are taking GCSE's and A-Levels in languages, and fewer universities are offering language courses. This highlights the extent to which languages are being forgotten and pushed aside. People are no longer given the same levels of opportunity to study languages compared to several years ago.

The history of the world's languages is largely based solely on loss and decline. The way in which languages are dying out, it will be no surprise that by 2100, half of the languages that currently exist, will be gone. Although said languages would probably be recorded in an archive somewhere, the thought of half the languages that we see today would be gone, is a scary thought.

It can be argued that without spiritual transformations, there cannot be social transformations. They are both interlinked in regards to how society changes and evolves through generation to generation. Language responds and transforms in association with the social, economic and political factors of society, that ultimately change the way we speak. New places, roles, powers, culture and ideologies, gain recognition whilst older ones die out, or simply gain new meaning.

Question 5

In the first paragraph, what factor is the decline of languages linked with?

A – Political causes.
B – The development of language.
C – Urbanisation.
D – An effect becoming a cause.
E – Spiritual transformation.

Answer

Question 6

The author uses the term 'sentimental archaism' to mean…

A – The retention of the old and obsolete.
B – Struggling to come to terms with the changes of language.
C – Understanding the influential factors of language.
D – Struggling to hold on to the past for sentimental reasons.
E – Identifying the social transformations of society.

Answer

Question 7

The author would *most* likely agree that...

A – Initial failures leads to more failures.

B – All language declines for political reasons.

C – Imprecise use of language is likely to make it more difficult to comprehend.

D – Social changes in our language is a direct cause from schooling systems.

E – The English language is a cause for concern.

Answer [   ]

3. Developmental Psychology

Developmental psychology is a useful way of determining the impact that social, biological and emotional factors can have on a person. A significant proportion of studies are conducted during childhood because children are at a stage where they are emotionally unstable, inexperienced and undergoing constant changes and developments.

I recently took it upon myself to ensure that I had a clear understanding of developmental psychology and the profound effects that early development can have on a child. In order to do this, I observed several children. This helped me to develop an analysis of how certain social factors within the home environment can lead to particular behavioural patterns. In particular, I studied the traits of children who grow up in a single parent household.

When studying the development of a child, there are two key developmental areas which must be considered. These are normative, and idiographic development. Combined, they form a cumulative process which seeks to establish the underlying reasons for the way a child behaves. Behaviour can often alter depending on the situation that the child is faced with, and it is these idiomatic changes in behaviour that are often the most valuable to psychological and developmental studies.

During my assessment, I mostly observed mothers and their children in the home. One situation occurred where a child had a noticeably strong attachment to his mother, who had raised him single-handedly without help from outsiders. There came a point where the mother had to leave the house for a number of hours, and left the child with a babysitter. Whilst the boy had known the babysitter for most of his life; his well-behaved, social and polite behaviour changed from the moment his mother left the house. He returned to his room, and stayed there for most of the day. Ignorant of my presence, I watched him pull the sheets off both his mother's and his own bed, and then build himself a fort. He surrounded himself with ornaments that belonged to him and his mother. He remained in the fort of memories until his mother returned; and then emerged as the polite, social and happy boy that he had been before she left.

While the satisfaction of building the fort could only be known to the child himself, I believe that his game was an attempt to prolong his attachment with his mother, until she returned.

Question 8

In the passage, what does the author infer is the *main* reason for the child's behaviour?

A – The child is bored, and is trying to amuse himself.

B – The child is trying to hold on to his mother by creating a game that involves her, to some extent.

C – The child is unable to cope with his mother being away from the house for so long.

D – The child is acting out in order to gain attention.

E – The child uses the 'fort' as a way of escaping from his mother.

Answer

Question 9

The 'fort' acts as a metaphor for…

A – Blocking out the world.

B – Feeling protected and connected to his mother.

C – Creating a fun game.

D – Seeking attention from his mother.

E – Constructing an escape route.

Answer

Question 10

In the context of the passage, what does the author mean by 'idiographic developments'?

A – The typical patterns of change.
B – Discovery of scientific facts in relation to childhood development.
C – The individual variations in patterns of change.
D – The perspectives of childhood development.
E – The study of childhood development.

Answer

Question 11

The position that the author takes in relation to the views of single-parents and the impact this has on children, is…

A – Fully against single-parent families.
B – Somewhat against single-parent families.
C – Neutral.
D – Somewhat supportive of single-parent families.
E – Fully supportive of single-parent families.

Answer

4. Freedom

A The terms 'free' and 'freedom' can often be related to an emotional state rather than a rational and meaningful term. Freedom is a word used in a wide variety of contexts, but the power of freedom of speech remains highly controversial.

B. Freedom of speech is a dangerous concept. The fact that people could be given the opportunity to spout racist, nationalist, derogatory or homophobic remarks can lead to unnecessary and substantiated abuse, which results in wider issues of cultural and social indifference.

C. It is no surprise that freedom of speech enrages some people. It is an emotional topic that highlights the importance of rights within democratic societies. The basis for democracy comes with a great sense of freedom and the ability to speak one's mind is continuously contested. However, it is important that free speech does not become hate speech, and is not used to incite or encourage violent behaviour. Free speech should be used as a means of illustrating the importance of personal rights and freedoms.

D. The term "speech" is a word full of emotion. A word full of anger, sadness, joyfulness or happiness; a term of endearment that allows a person to express themselves in a way that may be challenging to other views. We live in a world where we are simultaneously taught to be 'emotional' and 'speak our minds'. These expressions are taught to us in early childhood. Freedom of speech provides us with the opportunity to be an individual – something that all of us are taught. How then, can we be expected to retract our opinions and views on the basis that they might upset somebody? Are we not individuals who maintain the right to say what we think despite the consequences? It should not be restricted because of the careless mind-set of others, who express themselves through harsh language that is often considered wrong.

E. The idea of freedom of speech is difficult to debate due to the extent to which it can be defined, debated and controlled. Full freedom of speech is highly debated, and this constant need to determine which view point is right is ineffective, and will never be agreed. As a strong believer of the First Amendment, I find it difficult to place myself in a position which contests the use of vile language, but also the right to express yourself through language. People often ask 'how can you believe in the First Amendment, when you also believe swearing, racist and homophobic remarks should not be tolerated, despite the impact on individual choice?' A fair question, and a question that I simply cannot answer. There is a thin line between choosing to believe in something, and believing in it for the right reasons. I choose to follow the rules of the First Amendment, whilst still remaining holistically embedded in my own personal beliefs, and what I deem to be the acceptable.

Question 12

What is the *main* argument that author D is trying to make?

A – Freedom of speech is an emotive use of language that makes us who we are.

B – Freedom of speech is about individual expressions that teach us the importance of right from wrong.

C – Freedom of speech is about emotive language that can be seen as harmful to others.

D – Freedom of speech is a controversial debate and we must take it in our stride to accept opposing views to the social norm.

E – Freedom of speech is a far-fetched concept that can only be linked to the emotional state of an individual.

Answer

Question 13

Which authors would agree that freedom of speech is *not* about political aspects, but instead is a way of communicating a poignant response?

A – Author B and author C.

B – Author A and author C.

C – Author D and author E.

D – Author A and author D.

E – None of them.

Answer

Question 14

Which author, or authors, would be *most* inclined to agree that it is a violation of freedom of speech, to not be able to voice your opinions?

A – Author A.

B – Author B and C.

C – Author C.

D – Author D.

E – Author D and author E.

Answer

5. The Mentally Unstable and Prison Cells

The United States is said to have the highest rate of incarceration amongst all other developed countries. With over 2 million adults currently being held in jails and/or prisons; concerns over the number of adult offenders with mental instabilities has escalated.

There are numerous amounts of 'ill-offenders' who are obtained in prisons. These mentally ill offenders are simply considered highly irrational. This shows a lack of understanding regarding their behaviour.

Due to a lack of programmes such as rehabilitation, more and more people are entering prison cells as a substitute for intervention. This is disgraceful. The fact that the mentally unstable are being placed in prisons instead of receiving beneficiary help, is appalling.

Committing a crime is morally and socially wrong, that is without need for debate. But to imprison a person who shows high levels of mental instability not only puts pressure on the criminal justice system, but also puts pressure on the individual. By no means of their own, they have committed a crime that they might not have, had they been in the right mental capacity.

Mentally ill offenders are statistically shown to be more likely to commit violent crimes, such as murder, sexual assault and robbery, than those who are more mentally stable. These offences are dramatically higher in mentally ill prisoners by more than 10%. Surely this has something to do with the mental well-being of an individual? If a person *is not* in the right mind-set, and is in no control of his or her actions, should they be convicted on the same principles as a person *who is* in full control of his or her actions, and knows what they are doing? The notion that everyone is treated equally is good in principle, yet the circumstances of each individual are somewhat different, and should be taken into account.

In my opinion, the criminal justice system needs to appoint a new punishment system for ill-minded offenders. At the moment, when a person commits a crime, they are to be reprimanded, and this is done by way of deterrence. However, what is not taken into account is the difference between a person who is fully aware of their actions, and those who are not. To be deterred, a person needs to be fully aware and rational. They need to be fully aware of their actions to learn that those actions have consequences, and therefore must be punished.

However, a person with mental instabilities is in no control of their state of mind and therefore has no understanding of what their actions entail. In no way am I saying that ill-minded offenders should be given a free pass, I'm simply stating they should be assessed differently, and face deterrents which are decided on that basis.

Question 15

Which of the following *most* accurately captures the main inference of the passage?

A – Mentally ill offenders should be treated in other institutions such as a hospital instead of a prison.

B – All offences have consequences.

C – The point of prison is not for rehabilitation, it is for reprimand.

D – People should be sent to prison only as a last resort.

E – People who are deterred, should always be placed in imprisonment.

Answer [ ]

Question 16

Which of the following is an *unarticulated assumption*?

A – It does not give a clear depiction of what constitutes to being 'mentally unstable'.

B – The criminal justice system gives little room for manoeuvre in terms of punishment.

C – The lack of utilization is a cause for more people entering prison.

D – Mentally ill-offenders have no awareness regarding their actions.

E – Those who cannot be deterred, should not be imprisoned.

Answer [ ]

Question 17

Which of the following is an *opinion* rather than *fact*?

A – 'Committing a crime is morally and socially wrong...'

B – 'Circumstances of each individual are somewhat different and should be taken into account'.

C – 'With over 2 million adults currently being held in jails and/or prisons...'

D – 'These offences are dramatically higher in mentally ill prisoners by more than 10%...'

E – 'A person with mental instabilities is in no control of their state of mind...'

Answer

Question 18

In the passage, the writer *does not claim* that...

A – People with mental instabilities should be treated differently in the criminal justice system.

B – Imprisonment is a form of punishment.

C – The rehabilitation process for ill-offenders needs to incorporate the emotional well-being of an individual.

D – People deserve the opportunity for retribution.

E – Lack of health programmes are a result of the increased number of inmates.

Answer

6. Should teenagers be allowed to vote in elections?

A The proposal to allow younger teenagers to vote in elections is another attempt to turn adolescents into premature adults. Teenagers need time to mature and engage with 'real world' experiences; they have no clear understanding of what the 'real world' entails, nor can they comprehend the importance of making life changing decisions. It is thought that teenagers should be able to partake in society 100%, because at this age they are able to make life changing decisions such as leaving home, fighting to serve their country and getting married. Amidst these decisions comes great responsibility; a responsibility that affects only themselves, and therefore by no means should this stand as a reason to allow them to vote in political matters, which ultimately affect everyone on a national level.

B. Once a teenager has developed both emotionally and intellectually, only then should they be allowed to vote. A teenager is already going through numerous changes in terms of emotional maturity and puberty. They do not have the time, maturity, experience or intellect to be able to generate informed decisions that will subsequently affect the world in which we live. Teenagers do not need the responsibility to make important decisions such as voting. They're naive, immature and emotionally unstable.

C. If the children are our future, shouldn't they be given the opportunity to have an equal say? Teenagers are going to grow up in a world where important decisions are made regarding their future, and it is only fair that they too, have a say about what goes on. Teenagers are led to believe that their future is up to them, but denying them the choices and opportunities to express their views about their *own* future, marks a perverse way of limiting their responsibility.

D. Most teenagers are not fully informed in regards to political, economical and social conventions of society. They are simply uninterested in politics, general elections and voting. Government issues, healthcare, unemployment and other disputes founded in general elections are of a foreign language to teenagers. They do not comprehend what these issues *really* mean, nor do they maintain an understanding of what it takes to make informed decisions regarding such issues. Letting children become involved in politics will be as useless as a gun without a trigger.

E. It is time to change the age limit of voting. Teens are able to work, pay taxes and support families. They can be sent to prison or leave home, become independent, have a baby, and not rely on anyone else, and yet they cannot vote. Why can't they vote? Because of this insane notion that they are irresponsible and immature. Yet children are growing up faster in today's society. With the help of social media, news stories and television debates, they are fast becoming more aware of worldly events than anyone gives them credit for.

Question 19

Which author (A, B, C, D or E) uses a simile to elaborate on the implications of teenagers votes within society?

A – Author A.
B – Author B.
C – Author C.
D – Author D.
E – Author E.

Answer [   ]

Question 20

In paragraph D, the author claims that issues of general debate are of a *'foreign language'* to teenagers. The author uses this term to…

A – Demonstrate the importance of language within political debates.
B – Put emphasis on the role of general elections and the importance of its final decisions.
C – Highlight their lack of knowledge and ability to understand the nature of elections.
D – Suggest that teenagers are too emotionally unstable to fully comprehend the demands of voting.
E – Illustrate that teenagers are already making important life changing decisions.

Answer [   ]

Question 21

Which author (A, B, C, D or E) uses a counter-argument, in order to dismiss it as irrelevant?

A – Author A.
B – Author B.
C – Author C.
D – Author D.
E – Author E.

Answer

7. Do We Need Speed Cameras?

The use of speed cameras are often justified on the grounds that 'speed kills'. Thus, any preventative measures used to reduce the risk of death can only be seen as a positive.

The number of offenders caught on camera and fined in 2013 was over 115,000 within the UK and Wales. This is the highest figure recorded since 2009. In 2011, the number of speeding fines was over 110,000. While only 30% of road crashes are actually associated with speed and dangerous driving, excessive speed is found to play a significant part in all of those crashes, and 2010 saw around 200 deaths that related to speeding. This proves that speed cameras do not deter people from speeding. Millions of offenders are caught on camera each year, and new evidence suggests that the use of speed cameras is simply not reducing accidents. Moreover, arguments suggest that speed cameras are becoming more and more ineffective, and possibly influencing bad driving as opposed to solving it.

Speed cameras should be removed and then re-introduced with good police patrols. Figures from the Department of Transport indicate that only 5% of all fatal accidents are connected with excessive speeding. Speed cameras are unable to record factors such as road conditions, drunk drivers, misjudging distances, and failing to indicate; yet all of these are more of a cause for concern than excessive speed.

Police patrols are a more reliable safety precaution that would implement a strategy that would take into consideration all the important road safety factors, including speed. Unlike speed cameras, police patrols are more likely to reduce the number of records regarding incidents of dangerous driving, whether that is from dangerous driving or other factors such as the weather and road conditions.

Speed cameras are considered a highly ineffective and troublesome measure for most drivers. You may be driving safely, leaving a reasonable gap between your car and the car in front, adhering to the speed limit, paying attention to what's going on around you; but this is pointless if you get some other car who spots a speed camera and brakes instantly in order to reduce their speed. Clearly this affects the safety of not only that driver, but other nearby drivers.

The fixed speed camera acts as a visual reminder that at some point in the past, someone made a fatal roadside mistake. Nowadays, this is not always the case; although it still sometimes is an affective safety precaution. The best road safety precaution is us, the driver. Speed cameras have been placed in areas where fatal accidents were not previously an issue, yet the Government has issued the implementation of speed cameras as a way of 'managing risk'. What risk? If there was no risk to begin with, what is the point of the speed camera being there? All they do is affect the concentration of the driver and reduce the driver's attention to risk by already establishing a 'supposedly' dangerous area, which may or may not have been a place of an accident in the past.

Question 22

In paragraph two, the author uses evidence of the number of fines in 2013 for speeding to claim that cameras do not stop people from speeding. What is the *underlying assumption* in regards to this piece of evidence?

A – At the current rate, speed cameras will catch double that in 2013.

B – The number of speed cameras has remained the same over the years.

C – Speed cameras are ineffective.

D – Speed cameras are only cost effective.

E – The number of drivers driving irresponsibility has increased as a direct result of speed cameras.

Answer

Question 23

Identify the *main* conclusion of paragraph three.

A – Speed cameras are a safety hazard.

B – We should not rely on speed cameras to determine our speed.

C – Speed cameras act as a roadside visual reminder of safety.

D – Speed cameras should be replaced with police patrols.

E – The use of speed cameras can be justified.

Answer

Question 24

In paragraph two, the author uses a counter-argument to…

A – Strengthen the main argument, by dismissing the counter-argument.
B – Elaborate on the argument in which the author is trying to make.
C – Provide an equal account for both the pros and cons.
D – Highlight the importance of using speed cameras as a safety precaution.
E – To convey both sides of the argument.

Answer

Question 25

Which word in the passage is *not* used to demonstrate the dangers of speed cameras?

A – 'Clearly…'
B – '…affect…'
C – '…yet…'
D – 'although…'
E – 'Millions…'

Answer

8. Children and Crime

Police statistics for 2013 showed that approximately 34,600 youngsters between the ages of 10 (the age of criminal responsibility) and 17, had been convicted of a crime. Child crime is undoubtedly out of control. More than 120 primary school children were convicted in 2013, and 40 of those had been in trouble with the law at least once before.

During 2006, a record of 3,000 crimes were conducted in England and Wales by children under the age of 10. 10! An age where you are so innocent and naïve that you could not possibly comprehend getting into trouble with the law.

It is argued that the majority of these crimes are acts of minor damage such as criminal damage, graffiti, or shop-lifting. Surely it is not acceptable to categorise children as 'criminals'. By all accounts, it is nothing more than childhood 'naughtiness'. Such incidents are only recorded because of Government incentives to collect statistical data regarding offences that can then be used for analysis for future reference.

Children under the age of 10 cannot be prosecuted because they are under the age of criminal responsibility. When an offence is committed by someone under the age of 10, they cannot receive any formal outcome. The preventative measures for children's behaviour are practically non-existent, with only minor preventative measures in place to tackle crime in regards to the younger generation.

The use of ASBO's is a successful tool to tackle yobbish behaviour. Anti-social behaviour orders (ASBO's) are a civil order given to a person who has shown and engaged in some form of anti-social behaviour. Anyone over the age of 10 can be given an ASBO, this means they are restricted to doing certain things. The ASBO usually lasts for 2 years, during which it can be reviewed pending on behaviour. However, the fact that ASBO's can only be given to youngsters who are of criminal responsibility, means that there is still no method for punishing those under that age.

It is about time that institutions of power got involved and reduced the minimum age for ASBO's. The facts already show how children under the age of 10 are becoming more and more involved in some form of crime, and without a punishment in place, children will continue to re-offend. Introducing a similar ASBO for children under the age of 10 could prevent youngsters from the age of 5 from committing crimes. Not only would this ASBO work as a type of punishment, but it would also provide those in desperate need of it; with structure, discipline and care.

Question 26

In context of paragraph 4, what does the term 'age of criminal responsibility' mean in the sentence *'children under the age of 10 cannot be prosecuted because they are under the age of criminal responsibility?'*

A – They are not of age to be arrested or charged with any crime.

B – Their crimes are seen as less offensive, and action is not necessary.

C – They are not allowed to be held accountable for their actions.

D – They show no remorse for their actions.

E – None of the above.

Answer

Question 27

In the passage, the author *implies*, but does not state, that…

A – Youth offences are becoming out of control.

B – The Government have done little to tackle youth offences.

C – Youth offences will continue to increase.

D – ASBO's for younger children can be used as a rehabilitation process.

E – Child offenders under the age of 10 should be imprisoned, just like other offenders.

Answer

Question 28

Which of the following words from the passage, is used to convey a stereotypical representation of children?

A – '...naughtiness'.
B – '...naïve'.
C – '...minor'.
D – '...yobbish'.
E – '...innocent'.

Answer

9. Search Engines

The internet has become a universal medium, and it is the conduit for most of the information that we now receive. The internet uses a technique which has been designed so that the most relevant content is placed at the top of page listings, and ultimately narrows down your searches. This manipulation of search engine sites and controlled ranking, is done through a process called "search engine optimisation". It allows certain websites or webpages to be visible on the top ranking pages, and makes them more likely to appear in search results, resulting in higher numbers of visitors.

Search engines offer an array of online advertising services, searches and software tools. They offer online productivity including emails, cloud storage space, office suites and documents, and even social networking services. With libraries in decline, and books being considered 'old-fashioned', media platforms seem to make perfect sense. But are search engines dumbing us down? Theorists have argued how in today's society, the media is the cause of fragmented perceptions of the truth, via misleading and incorrect information.

Critics are urging teachers at all levels of education to equip students with the right skills and knowledge to be able to sift through and interpret information found online, and assess its plausibility. There is no doubt that the decrease in libraries and books, and the increase in advanced technology, has led to a culture so indulged with the internet, that they struggle to differentiate between anecdotal and unsubstantiated material that is posted online.

Some search engines contain articles on pretty much any information you would want, but are riddled with flaws. The fact that these websites are contributor-based, i.e. anyone can post and edit pages, means that they are often criticised for containing mistakes, and this plays an important role in the dumbing down of contemporary culture. Search engines make it acceptable to publish information that everyone can access, in spite of being inaccurate.

The internet is subsequently producing a generation of people who are digesting unreliable information, that is often used in studies and research. People who use the internet can be described as "a sponge". They are taught to absorb information through extensive research. However, what they fail to realise is that the information they are absorbing needs to be considered in terms of accuracy. Online sources are often unreliable, contain shallow ideas and are defective. Students need to be able to sieve through information from the internet, and determine what is accurate and what is superficial. Critics are concerned with students plagiarising their work. Students need to understand the importance of the internet, the affect that it has on academia, and the importance of gaining correct information and data from online sources.

Question 29

Using the metaphor of "a sponge" *mainly* suggests that…

A – The internet is full of useful information.

B – The internet is full of information, and this is being absorbed by its users.

C – Students are too naïve to determine reliable sources.

D – The internet does not offer any valuable information.

E – Students should not be able to use the internet in their academic studies.

Answer

Question 30

The *main* argument that the author is trying to make is…

A – Online information is incorrect.

B – Online information cannot be trusted.

C – Students plagiarise their work from online information.

D – Students use online information extensively.

E – The material on the internet lacks no authority.

Answer

Question 31

In the first paragraph, the author discusses SEO and rankings. What is the author trying to illustrate?

A – There is too much information on the internet.
B – Certain search engines gain profit from using SEO.
C – Rankings are not always reliable.
D – There is not enough regulation on the internet.
E – All the good content is ranked higher up.

Answer

Question 32

In the second paragraph, the author highlights how the media is shattering facts and truths, in order to…

A – Strengthen his argument of how society is 'dumbing down'.
B – Illustrate a counter-argument, in order to dismiss an opposing idea.
C – Highlight the important benefits of the internet.
D – Strengthen the idea of search engines becoming a cultural phenomenon.
E – Provide an example of how search engines are profitable.

Answer

10. Civics, Citizenship and Students

Civics is the study of the theoretical and practical aspects of citizenship. Ultimately, civics refers to the way in which citizens are educated. The branch of political science demonstrates the social rights and responsibilities which are inflicted upon us in order to maintain a stable and effective society. They are used to form ideologies which allow us to understand acceptable norms of behaviour, attitude and values.

Civic virtues and even civility, are in decline. Not only that, but the civil and moral qualities associated with good citizenship are also in decline. Students are being taught citizenship in a dry and abstract manner, and are expected to engage with the political and precedential constitutions of the period in which we live.

Students often experience a feeling of disconnection between theory that is taught and real life practice. Students are sceptical about things they read because they live in a world full of discontent, objection, anger and conflict. How can they be expected to divulge into textbook theory and comprehend good citizenship, when nothing proves this to be the case? It is no wonder that students find the notion of civics boring, hypocritical and somewhat corrupt.

A major deficiency in regards to both civic education and government, is the sheer lack of understanding of fundamental values, principles and views on democracy and constitutionalism. This knowledge is needed to provide the basic foundations of society. It is the pioneer to the reasoning and commitments of citizens in regards to democratic solutions.

Representatives of government power illustrate how citizenship necessitates the knowledge about government issues and the ability to become involved in all things governance. It means knowing how to identify and inform yourself about issues, explore and evaluate possible solutions, and then act to resolve these problems. It demands that you know how to interact respectfully with others, in order to convey good citizenship. In turn, young people who are more familiar with the concepts of civics, will be more inclined to encourage civic action and participate in voting, contacting Governments, discussing political issues and emerge themselves in social and political disputes.

However, these constant attempts to demonstrate the importance of citizenship are somewhat futile. The benefits of providing good citizenship are undeniable, and still many people choose to disobey or challenge the common rules and regulations set by governments. What then, is the purpose of continuing civic action if less and less people choose to follow it? The younger generation will ultimately be the future of our society. They are so wrapped up with rebellious behaviour against rules and government proceedings that they choose to follow their own path, in a country that is passionate about political engagements.

Question 33

In what context is the word 'disconnection' used within paragraph three?

A – The inability of civic values founded within society.

B – The attitude in which critics believe students lack the knowledge of being good citizens.

C – The inability to differentiate between good and bad behaviour.

D – To highlight the attitude that students have towards theoretical and practical understandings of citizenship.

E – The importance of civic values and how this maintains an effective society.

Answer

Question 34

What is the *underlying assumption* in paragraph three?

A – Teaching theory is too complex for students.

B – Living practice makes it easier for students to apply theoretical understandings.

C – Students believe theory is useless.

D – Teaching theory is difficult to apply to living practice.

E – Students find theoretical civics boring.

Answer

Question 35

Why does the author believe that attempts to demonstrate the importance of citizenship are 'futile?'

A – The younger generation would rather take drugs.

B – Citizenship is an outdated concept.

C – Citizenship cannot be demonstrated.

D – Citizenship is boring.

E – The younger generation would rather follow their own path than take citizenship lessons.

Answer

11. The Worrying Increase of Health Supplements

A recent study has illustrated that dietary supplements have become increasingly popular, with more than half of all adults in America taking some form of health supplement.

The use of health supplements such as multivitamin tablets are regularly used as an "insurance policy" to ensure that you are receiving all of the necessary nutrients. The increased usage of such supplements has become apparent within the western world, which advertises the prevention of a range of medical conditions. The central issue is not with the supplements that are being used, but that they are being taken in high dosages.

People are already taking too many pills due to increased health problems, often caused by unhealthy diets. People take these pills instead of adopting healthier lifestyle choices, thus believing it will 'fix' their health problems. In 2012, it was estimated that 72 million prescriptions were placed for paracetomol, plus another 78 million for stronger paracetomol containing codeine.

Research indicates that people who take supplements for Vitamin C of over 5000 milligrams per day, are more at risk of developing cancer. Health supplements, despite the constant advertising of health benefits, are shown to be causing both short-term and long-term health issues.

Despite being labelled 'natural', over 90% of these supplements are synthetic, and new research indicates that they could be doing more harm than good. People use these supplements to replace the consumption of food. Supplements are not a food replacement. They should not be consumed on the basis that it is 'easier' and more 'time-efficient' than preparing and eating a meal.

The need for a ban on certain health supplements needs to be carefully considered before instigating preventative measures. Some may argue that this is an infringement on your freedom of rights. The freedom to choose what you do, what you take and how you live your life is up to you. Therefore intruding on an individual's rights and telling them what supplements they should or should not be taking, is frowned upon. For example, banning smoking in public places was frowned upon when it was first initiated, and yet we have since seen the exponential health benefits of banning smoking in public places. There are a plethora of instances where the government have made changes in order to better the interests of the overall public, for example setting road speed limits in order to ensure safety on the roads.

If health supplements are banned, this will make people naturally healthier. It will force them to purchase products such as fruit and vegetables, which they may not have consumed before the ban was enforced. Not only will this benefit the individual's health by providing them with natural minerals and nutrients, but it will also allow for improvements to be made to the economy.

Question 36

What is the *main* point that the author makes by comparing health supplements with road speed limits?

A – To demonstrate the dangers of speeding.

B – To encourage people to drive more carefully.

C – The Government enforce rules and regulations in order to serve the people's best interests.

D – To demonstrate how the Government highlights the importance of safety.

E – To show that the Government is only concerned with protecting their own assets.

Answer

Question 37

From the tone of the whole passage, which of the following do you think *best* describes the attitude of the author?

A – Doubting.

B – Dubious.

C – Disapproving.

D – Contemptible.

E – Manipulated.

Answer

Question 38

In the passage, which of the following words is *not* associated with the welfare of banning supplements?

A – '...preventative'.

B – '...synthetic'.

C – '...measures'.

D – '...benefits'.

E – '...natural'.

Answer

Question 39

Which word is *not* used to demonstrate the author's favour to ban health supplements?

A – '...interests'.

B – '...exponential'.

C – '...replacement'.

D – '...issue'.

E – '...frowned'.

Answer

12. Globular Clusters

Globular clusters are primarily made up of spherical collections of stars. These collaborations of stars orbit the galactic core as a type of 'satellite'. They are symmetrical systems formed about 13 billion years ago, and are described as the oldest remaining stellar subsystem within the galaxies.

The galaxy of the Milky Way is currently known to have 157 globular clusters, and these objects belong to the formation of the *halo*. When Harlow Shapley, one of the pioneers of astrology, first began his studies in relation to stars and globular clusters, little did he know about how the galaxy was formed.

New observations regarding globular clusters in the Milky Way have cast huge debates in the theory of how the galaxy formed. The stars that form the globular cluster of the Milky Way are believed to have formed during the formation of the galaxy itself. The conventional ideas circulating this theory contend that the Milky Way formed in a short space of time (approximately 200 million years). This is said to have formed due to a spherical cloud of gas that emerged as a result of the direct pressure involving gravity. This rapid formation of the galaxy suggests that the stars are likely to be around the same age.

Controversially, astronomer Michael Bolte considered other variations in the different ages of the globular clusters, and studied how one of the clusters is 2 billion years older than the other clusters in the galaxy.

With that in mind, astronomers began to re-evaluate their studies and took another look at other theories that could be evaluated. In the early 1970's, it was argued by Richard Larson that the halo of the galaxy was created across a billion or more years, as hundreds of small gas clouds drifted about and collided, to ultimately condense the elliptical system of the universe. His conceptions of "turbulent and lumpy" protogalaxy is complemented by thoughts of interacting spiral galaxies losing energy to merge as a single-formed assemble.

With the most powerful telescopes, it is possible to visually locate these clusters more precisely. The stars that make up most of the cluster tends to be of an older age, and can be classified by age in relation to the redness in colour. Stars nearer the disk, tend to be of a blue nature. The most prominent cluster that can be seen under a small telescope is M13, in the constellation of *Hercules*, which contains hundreds of thousands of stars.

Question 40

The word 'halo' is written in italics. In the context of paragraph two, what could you *assume*?

A – The stars appearance makes them look serene and idyllic.

B – It is the name of the founder of the clusters.

C – Surrounded by other galaxies which, all together, form a halo.

D – The clusters of the Milky Way are scattered in a sphere shape, forming an illusion of a *halo*.

E – Cannot be determined.

Answer

Question 41

The passage is predominantly concerned with…

A – Determining the age of the stars in the globular clusters of the Milky Way.

B – The history of the globular clusters and the significance of these collective stars.

C – Changes in the procedures used by astronomers to understand the formation.

D – Current debates between astronomers in regards to the correct theory of the formation of globular clusters.

E – The effect of new discoveries regarding the Milky Way and theories of globular clusters.

Answer

Question 42

In regards to Larson's conventional theory of the Milky Way, Larson *implies* that his theory differs by...

A – Assessing the size of the galaxy.

B – Determining the time it took for the Milky Way to form.

C – Demonstrating that particular gases contribute to the formation of the galaxy.

D – The shape of the galaxy.

E – Determining the age of the stars that form the globular cluster.

Answer

SECTION B – ESSAY QUESTION

Answer **one** of the following questions.

Your answer should be a reasoned and substantiated argument, which justifies your response to the question that you have chosen.

You have 40 minutes in which to draft and write your answer to one essay question.

1. What is equality? Does it really matter?

2. Make the best case for Government funding the arts programmes.

3. Why does 'political correctness' matter?

We have provided you with space to write out an answer or draft to the questions above. Additional paper may be required.

1. What is equality? Does it really matter?

2. Make the best case for Government funding the Arts programmes.

3. Why does 'political correctness' matter?

ANSWERS TO MOCK TEST

SECTION A – MULTIPLE-CHOICE

'Education Science and Society'

Q1. C = 'The current teaching system is not supportive for students who want to learn about the subject'.

EXPLANATION = the author is primarily discussing his concerns over the way science is being taught in schools, and how he believes the current system is not supportive for students who want to learn about the subject.

Q2. B = 'Contemptuous'.

EXPLANATION = within the third paragraph of the passage, the author talks about public and secondary schools in a way that is slightly disapproving and sneering of the educational system. The word 'contemptuous' can be used to define the author's snarling attitude towards the educational system in relation to the sciences.

Q3. C = 'Lack of direct experience' and E = 'Teaching methods'.

EXPLANATION = whilst all the answers listed seem reasonable enough, not all of them can be inferred from the passage. The author blames a lack of direct experience, and poor teaching methods, for the failure of educational science in schools.

Q4. B = 'It is relatively simple to learn the methods of scientific discoveries'.

EXPLANATION = the author makes several inferences throughout the passage, and out of the answer options available, the only inference the author does not make is that 'it is relatively simple to learn the methods of scientific discoveries'. In fact, the author makes the exact opposite inference throughout the passage by highlighting the difficult and complex task it is to fully understand the sciences.

'The Decline of Different Languages'

Q5. D = 'An effect becoming a cause'.

EXPLANATION = this question focuses on your ability to pick out what the example is referring to. You will notice that the author talks about effects and causes just before the example is mentioned. The example is given to elaborate on this point, and therefore reinforces the notion of effects vs. causes.

Q6. D = 'Struggling to hold on to the past for sentimental reasons'.

EXPLANATION = the use of the word 'sentimental' refers to the emotional attachment, rather than rationality. The word 'archaism' can be defined as 'a thing that is very old or old-fashioned; something presented or occurred from the past'. Therefore the most solid meaning for 'sentimental archaism' in the context of the passage is struggling to hold on to the past. In other words, there is an emotional attachment that makes it difficult to let go of something from the past.

Q7. C = 'Imprecise use of language is likely to make it more difficult to comprehend'.

EXPLANATION = the author implies in the passage that the use of language can affect the way in which we understand things. Thus, the author would most likely agree that "imprecise use of the language is likely to make it more difficult to comprehend", and thus effect the way in which we view and speak that language.

'Developmental Psychology'

Q8. B = 'The child is trying to hold on to his mother by creating a game that involves her, to some extent'.

EXPLANATION = the author uses a lot of claims and discusses developmental psychology in a variety of areas, but the question specifically asks for the main inference that is made, and within this passage it refers to the 'child trying to hold on to his mother by creating a game that involves her, to some extent'.

Q9. B = 'Feeling protected and connected to his mother'.

EXPLANATION = the use of the 'fort' acts as a metaphor of feeling protected and connected with his mother who, when isn't there, leaves the child feeling somewhat lost.

Q10. C = 'The individual variations in patterns of change'.

EXPLANATION = in relation to the passage, the term 'idiographic developments' means "the individual variations in the patterns of change". Unlike normative developments, whereby it refers to the typical changes that would likely be encountered, idiographic developments is used to suggest changes that are unusual or deviate from the norm.

Q11. C = 'Neutral'.

EXPLANATION = you cannot determine the position in which the author takes. The author does not claim any particular view in regards to whether or not they believe single-parent families have a profound effect on children. The author states several claims but does not elaborate on personal belief, so therefore the author must take a neutral view in regards to developmental psychology.

'Freedom'

Q12. A = 'Freedom of speech is an emotive use of language that makes us who we are'.

EXPLANATION = out of all the possible answer options, only answer A can be concluded from author D's discussion. Author D speaks about the importance of emotions and expressions which make up an individual. Therefore option A seems the only logical answer that concludes the author's viewpoints.

Q13. D = 'Author A and author D'.

EXPLANATION = authors A and D both express freedom of speech as being an emotive tool of communication. Whilst author C also discusses the importance of emotion, they do so by involving political discussions as well, and this does not answer the question. Authors A and D both use emotion as a way of discussing how a person can express their views based on their beliefs, moral and sense of individual interpretation.

Q14. D = 'Author D'.

EXPLANATION = only author D would be *most* inclined to agree that it is a violation of freedom of speech to not be able to voice your opinions in public. None of the other authors show a strong belief that it is a violation. Author A does not take a view side in regards to freedom of speech; they merely state facts. Author C discusses how freedom of speech "encourages violent behaviour", so therefore could not agree to the statement proposed. Author B holds freedom of speech to be a dangerous concept, that goes against the ideas mentioned in the passage. Author E shows a discussion based on good and bad points regarding freedom of speech, and therefore would not likely be most inclined to agree with the proposed statement.

'The Mentally Unstable and Prison Cells'

Q15. A = 'Mentally ill offenders should be treated in other institutions such as a hospital instead of a prison'.

EXPLANATION = answer option A most accurately captures the main inference in which the author is trying to convey throughout the passage. The main interpretation that can be taken from the reading is that mentally ill offenders need to have a different rehabilitation process as opposed to people who are fully aware of their actions.

Q16. B = 'The criminal justice system gives little room for manoeuvre in terms of punishment'.

EXPLANATION = an unarticulated assumption can be defined as an unspoken conjecture. In other words, something that can be guessed or assumed, but is not verbally stated. Answer option B demonstrates an unspoken assumption. The passage indicates that the criminal justice system gives no room manoeuvre in terms of punishment. This is not stated, but the fact that everyone is treated the same in terms of punishment, suggests that it is difficult to challenge the fixed imprisoning sentence, despite the circumstances of an individual.

Q17. B = 'Circumstances of each individual are somewhat different, and should be taken into account'.

EXPLANATION = out of the answer options available, the only answer that demonstrates the author's opinion is that the "circumstances of each individual are somewhat different, and should be taken into account". All of the other answers demonstrate statistical or factual information.

Q18. D = 'People deserve the opportunity for retribution'.

EXPLANATION = within the passage, the writer does not claim that "people deserve the opportunity for retribution". This is the opposite of what the author is trying to argue.

'Should Teenagers Be Allowed To Vote?'

Q19. D = 'Author D'.

EXPLANATION = author D uses the simile 'letting children become involved in politics will be as useless as a gun without a trigger'. No other author uses a simile to emphasis their discussion, so answer option A is correct.

Q20. C = 'Highlight the lack of knowledge and ability to understand the nature of elections'.

EXPLANATION = the use of the term 'foreign language' in relation to teenagers and politics is used to highlight the lack of knowledge and ability to understand the nature of elections. Answer A can be ruled out because there is no clear link between the term and the 'importance of language' within political debates. Answer B can be ruled out because the term is not used to emphasise the importance of general elections. It has no clear link to the term 'foreign language'. Answer D can be ruled out because paragraph D does not mention anything about emotions in relation to foreign language. Answer E can be ruled out because the term is not used to illustrate the important decisions teenagers are already making; the term 'foreign language' is used to suggest that teenagers are not familiar with the demanding nature in which voting entails.

Q21. A = 'Author A'.

EXPLANATION = Author A uses the counter-argument of the 'thought that teenagers should be able to partake in society 100%, because, and at this age, they already can make life changing decisions such as leaving home, fighting to serve their country and get married'. This is a counter-argument of the main argument in which the author is trying to make; that teenagers are not ready to be given the opportunity to vote in general elections.

'Do We Need Speed Cameras?'

Q22. B = 'The number of speed cameras has remained the same over the years'.

EXPLANATION = the underlying assumption of the evidence needs to be that the number of speed cameras has remained the same over the years. Without this assumption, you would not be able to draw upon the same conclusion. If the number of speed cameras differentiated each year, the statistics would not remain as effective.

Q23. D = 'Speed cameras should be replaced with police patrols'.

EXPLANATION = the main conclusion that can be established in paragraph 3 is that speed cameras should be replaced with police patrols. Answer A can be ruled out because this is a generalised statement and is too vague to form a strong conclusion. Answer B can be ruled out because it is not discussed within the paragraph, and therefore cannot conclude the paragraph. Answers C and E do work as conclusions, however, they do not conclude paragraph 3, and therefore are not correct.

Q24. A = 'Strengthen the main argument, by dismissing the counter-argument'.

EXPLANATION = the idea of using a counter-argument, for any author, is to be able to make their argument stronger, by dismissing opposing viewpoints. Therefore the correct answer would be (A).

Q25. D = '...although'

EXPLANATION = the word 'although' is used in the last paragraph, to counter argue the use of speed cameras. This word is not used to demonstrate the dangers of speed cameras, and instead illustrates a benefit of using speed cameras.

'Children and Crime'

Q26. A = 'They are not old enough to be arrested or charged with any crime'.

EXPLANATION = in context of the passage, the term 'age of criminal responsibility' refers to the age that children are not able to be arrested or charged with any crimes because they are under the 'age of criminal responsibility', which, as it stands is 10 years old.

Q27. D = 'ASBO's for young children can be used as a rehabilitation process'.

EXPLANATION = the author implies, but does not state that ASBO's can be used as a rehabilitation process. The author discusses several reasons as to why child ASBO's should be enforced.

Q28. D = '...yobbish'.

EXPLANATION = the only word out of the answer options available which is used to stereotype young children who commit crimes and show anti-social behaviour is 'yobbish'.

'Search Engines'

Q29. B = 'The internet is full of information, and is absorbed by its users'.

EXPLANATION = in context of the passage, the use of the term "sponge", suggests that online resources are full of information in which are minds are able to 'absorb'. However, this information does not necessarily offer nutritional or beneficial content. For example, the passage indicates that the internet is an online service that contains contributions by its users, therefore this messes with validity of the information that can be found on the internet.

Q30. D = 'Students use online information extensively'.

EXPLANATION = the main argument in which the author is trying to make throughout the passage is that "students use online information extensively". In other words, students have become so reliant on the information founded online, that this is the only information that they know, regardless of whether it is correct or not.

Q31. C = 'Rankings are not always reliable'.

EXPLANATION = within the first paragraph, the author discusses SEO and ranking lists to illustrate that rankings are not always reliable. The fact that the author suggests search engine optimization can be used to alter and make web pages visible demonstrates the power of the internet, and how rankings are not produced in accordance to the *best* information, it is produced on how many *visitors* go to that page.

Q32. A = 'Strengthen this argument of how society is 'dumbing down'

EXPLANATION = the passage discusses the importance of the internet, and how this negatively effects the learning process of students who ultimately use the internet for most of their work. However, the fact that students use this service extensively, and are therefore using incorrect information, has led to a collective 'dumbing down' of society.

'Civics, Citizenship and Students'

Q33. D = 'To highlight the attitude that students have towards theoretical and practical understandings of citizenship'.

EXPLANATION = the term 'disconnection' is used in paragraph three to demonstrate the attitude which students have towards theoretical and practical understandings of citizenship. Students are not connected with the theoretical concepts of citizenship, nor are they experienced enough to fully understand the importance of practical civics in real life.

Q34. D = 'Teaching theory is difficult to apply to living practice'.

EXPLANATION = the underlying assumption with paragraph three is that teaching theory is difficult to apply to living practice. Living practice cannot be taught from a textbook, nor can it be taught by theory and knowledge, living practice is done through experiencing the real world for yourself and gaining your own view of society. The author demonstrates the importance of distinguishing between these two terms in order to elaborate on the importance of how civics can be achieved.

Q35. E = 'The younger generation would rather follow their own path than take citizenship lessons'.

EXPLANATION = the author clearly states that attempts to demonstrate the importance of citizenship are somewhat futile, due to the fact that the younger generation would rather follow their own path, and rebel against government rules and regulations.

'The Worrying Increase of Health Supplements'

Q36. C = 'The Government enforce rules and regulations in order to serve the people's best interests'.

EXPLANATION = the main point in which the author is trying to make by comparing health supplements to road safety is that rules and regulations are enforced in order to serve the people's best interests. Road speed limits are enforced to reduce the risk of accidents and provide safer driving, whereas the ban on health supplements will reduce health risks and provide a healthier, more natural lifestyle.

Q37. C = 'Disapproving'.

EXPLANATION = the author has a strong, disapproving attitude towards health supplements.

Q38. B = '...synthetic'

EXPLANATION = 'synthetic' is the word used that does not associate the benefits of taking health supplements. This term is used to show what the health supplements consist of, it is not a word used to show the benefits of banning supplements.

Q39. D = '...issue'

EXPLANATION = the word 'issue' in the passage is not used to demonstrate the author's belief in banning health supplements. Instead it is used in the context that 'the issue is not so much the supplements themselves, but the high dosage of these supplements that are being taken'.

'Globular Clusters'

Q40. D = 'The clusters of the Milky Way are scattered in a sphere shape, forming an illusion of a *halo*'.

EXPLANATION = the term *halo* is used to demonstrate how the clusters of the Milky Way are scattered in a sphere shape, forming an illusion of a halo. This makes the most sense within the context of the passage.

Q41. E = 'The effect of new discoveries regarding the Milky Way and theories of globular clusters'.

EXPLANATION = the passage is predominantly concerned with the effects of new discoveries and theories regarding the Milky Way and how this impacts our knowledge of globular clusters.

Q42. C = 'Demonstrating that particular gases contribute to the formation of the galaxy'.

EXPLANATION = according to the passage, Larson's argument differs in that it demonstrates that particular gases contribute to the formation of the galaxy, and therefore changes the way in which we view globular clusters and the formations of the galaxy.

SECTION B – ESSAY QUESTIONS

<u>1. What is equality? Does it really matter?</u>

This question can be broken down into two parts. Firstly, the question requires your ability to show an understanding and viewpoint regarding 'equality'. You will need to carefully structure your answer so that you answer this part of the question. Secondly, the question also requires you to demonstrate the importance of equality and whether it matters. This will allow you to illustrate your opinions and beliefs and elaborate on your thought process and the reasons behind it.

Below are some of the key points that you could include in order to strengthen your answer and provide a successful response.

Defining equality. Equality is about ensuring that every individual within every society has an equal opportunity. Equal opportunities include the rights to work, female and male equal rights, reduce discriminations in relation to sex, gender, race, religion, disabilities etc. Equality is a way of maintaining a standardised message within culture that opportunities need to be distributed equally, and not seen to benefit someone of particular interest.

History of equality. Within your essay, you could explain the history of equality, and how previous years have demonstrated a lack of equality amongst society, and how this has changed and evolved over time. Within contemporary society, we live in a world that is regulated and imposed with rules that prevent inequalities. However, you could argue that whilst regulations remain in place, inequality does still remain, and probably always will. Give an example of how people can challenge the current zeitgeist of society in relation to equality.

Significance. This is the second part of the question that you need to answer in order to gain high marks. You need to discuss the importance of equality and how this is important to culture. Inclusion, equality and opportunities are a central principle to building community capacity. Society needs a healthy and stable workforce, in order to create citizens who conform to the rules and regulations of society. What is the importance of equality in relation to democratic societies?

Equality and Diversity. Explain the relationship between equality and diversity and how this has a direct impact on the world we live in. For example, discuss approaches of how businesses, schools, religions and customs have changed over time in order to maintain diverse and current to the social norms of society.

Examples. It is important that when you make a claim, or suggestion, you try to back up your answer using examples and or evidence. Evidence does not have to be in the forms of statistics, but it will be useful if you can apply your claim to a situation that demonstrates what you are trying to say. For example, if you were discussing the importance of equality and referring to racial discrimination, you could apply it in a workforce scenario, and give reasons and responses to what effect this has and validate the point in which you are trying to make.

2. Make the best case for Government funding the arts programmes.

For this type of question, you need to adopt a view as to whether you are **for** or **against** the Government funding the arts programmes. You need to be able to create and highlight key points regarding the argument in which you decide to create, using sufficient examples and analysis to support your reasoning.

Below are some of the key points that you could include in order to strengthen your answer and provide a successful response.

Economic drive. The arts are a great way to create jobs. Jobs in relation to the arts programmes have become increasingly popular, and are part of a successful strategy in revitalising the economy. Arts and cultures are consistent factors of economic growth and increase economic development by attracting businesses, creating jobs, promoting tourism and generating revenue.

Educational benefits. The arts are a central focus point for the younger generation and facilitate success in schooling systems. Thus, art programmes enhance the overall capacity of a student's academic achievements in a range of subject areas including imagination, creative thinking, critical thinking, innovation and communication.

Arts are a hallmark. The arts provide a hallmark in state creative capacity and generate innovative and imaginative products and services. Any business or service can benefit greatly from creative ideas that take a place in the global marketplace.

Counter-argument. You could discuss the cons for Governments funding the arts programmes. You could discuss that jobs in the arts industry choose their jobs like other people choose their jobs. Therefore, you could suggest that people in the arts know the risk of choosing their profession, and should not be singled out from other jobs.

Arts are not a necessity. You could also discuss that the Government is already spending millions, and economies cannot afford to waste money on one particular area that may or may not be of success. The arts are not a necessity. They are a recreational element of society and therefore should not receive benefits funded by the Government to fund their recreation.

3. Why does 'political correctness' matter?

In order to answer this question, you need to have a solid understanding of what 'political correctness' means. This will form the first part of your essay. Then, you will need to analyse the importance of political correctness and determine whether or not it matters. You could argue that political correctness does not matter, but you will need to explain why and back up your answers. You can dismiss one view point as long as you explain why you have done this and provide a quality argument for the reasons you have chosen.

Definition. The first thing you need to include in your essay is a definition of political correctness. Political correctness is defined as a policy of being particularly careful not to upset or offend any groups within society. Political correctness avoids vocabulary that is often deemed, or may be seen as offensive, discriminatory or judgemental of others.

Conformism. You could argue how political correctness is a form of conformism and the social 'norm' which is expected from rule-abiding citizens. Political correctness is a narrowing of the range which we deem to be acceptable.

Coerce. Political correctness could be argued as coercing citizens and supressing any challenging opinion. This makes independent thought extremely restrictive, and removes a sense of individualism from society.

Why does it matter? The bulk of your essay should consider whether or not you believe political correctness to matter. Does it deepen our dishonesty? Are we subconsciously told to believe a certain thing, even if we have a different view on the matter?

Examples. It is important that your essay contains examples where appropriate, in order to enhance your argument and make it stronger. For example, you could show how certain 'humorous' stereotypes or jokes about a particular type of person are often made, despite this not being in line with political correctness. You could then discuss the potential repercussions of this, and also the moral implications concerning freedom of speech.

Term of abuse. People understand that it is a bad idea to offend or judge people. Thus, political correctness is intellectually dishonest, and sometimes incorrect. There is no system in place for a person who is politically correct to admit that he believes an offensive truth, and instead has to believe that the 'truth' behind the offense is not true and in fact, has to remain in denial.

A FEW
FINAL WORDS...

You have now reached the end of your Law National Admissions Testing guide and no doubt feel more prepared to tackle your LNAT. We hope you have found this guide an invaluable insight into the admissions test, and understand the expectations regarding your assessment.

For any type of test, we believe there are a few things to remember in order to better your chances and increase your overall performance.

REMEMBER – THE THREE P's!

1. **Preparation.** This may seem relatively obvious, but you will be surprised by how many people fail their assessment because they lacked preparation and knowledge regarding their test. You want to do your utmost to guarantee the best possible chance of succeeding. Be sure to conduct as much preparation prior to your assessment to ensure you are fully aware and 100% prepared to complete the test successfully. Not only will practising guarantee to better your chances of successfully passing, but it will also make you feel at ease by providing you with knowledge and know-how to pass your Law National Admissions Test.

2. **Perseverance.** You are far more likely to succeed at something if you continuously set out to achieve it. Everybody comes across times where there are setbacks or obstacles in the way of their goals. The important thing to remember when this happens, is to use those setbacks and obstacles as a way of progressing. It is what you do with your past experiences that helps to determine your success in the future. If you fail at something, consider 'why' you have failed. This will allow you to improve and enhance your performance for next time.

3. **Performance.** Your performance will determine whether or not you are likely to succeed. Attributes that are often associated with performance are *self-belief, motivation* and *commitment*. Self-belief is important for anything you do in life. It allows you to recognise your own abilities and skills and believe that you can do well. Believing that you can do well is half the battle! Being fully motivated and committed is often difficult for some people, but we can assure you that, nothing is gained without hard work and determination. If you want to succeed, you will need to put in that extra time and hard work!

Work hard, stay focused, and be what you want!

Good luck with your Law National Admissions Test. We would like to wish you the best of luck with all your future endeavours.

The How2become team

how2become

Get more books, manuals, online tests
and training courses at:

www.how2become.com